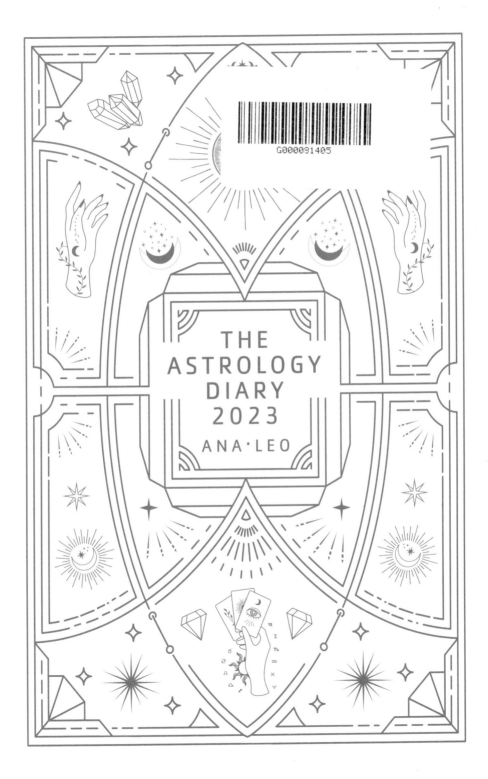

THE
ASTROLOGY
DIARY
2023

ANA·LEO

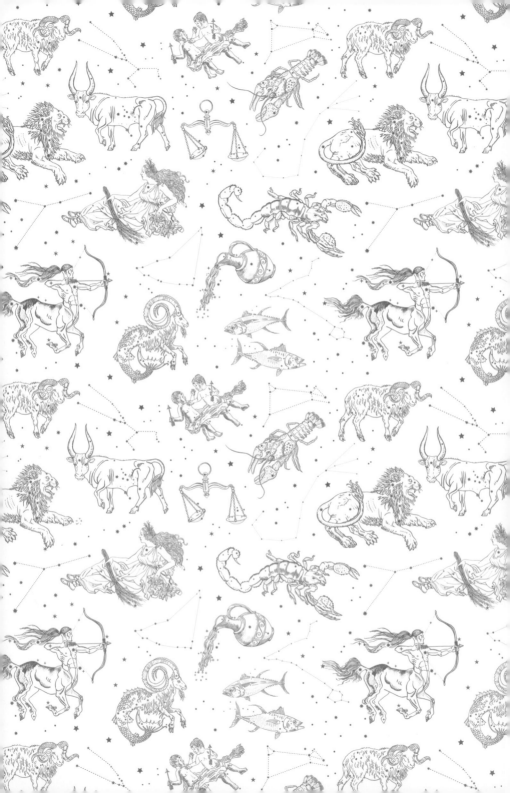

THE
ASTROLOGY
DIARY
2023

ANA·LEO

The Astrology Diary 2023

First published in UK and USA in 2022 by
Watkins, an imprint of Watkins Media Limited
Unit 11, Shepperton House, 89–93
Shepperton Road, London N1 3DF
enquiries@watkinspublishing.co.uk

Author: Ana Leo
Designer: Maria Clara Voegeli
Illustrations: Shutterstock
Commissioning Editor: Anya Hayes
Assistant Editor: Brittany Willis

ISBN: 978-178678-688-3

Printed in China

Signs of the Zodiac:

♒	Aquarius	January 20–February 17
♓	Pisces	February 18–March 19
♈	Aries	March 20–April 19
♉	Taurus	April 20–May 20
♊	Gemini	May 21–June 20
♋	Cancer	June 21–July 21
♌	Leo	July 22–August 22
♍	Virgo	August 23–September 21
♎	Libra	September 22–October 22
♏	Scorpio	October 23–November 21
♐	Sagittarius	November 22–December 20
♑	Capricorn	December 21–January 19

THIS DIARY BELONGS TO

NAME

DATE OF BIRTH   TIME

PLACE OF BIRTH   STATE

SOLAR SIGN   RISING SIGN

ADDRESS

CITY   STATE

COUNTRY

PHONE   MOBILE

EMAIL

WWW

🖒

🕊

📷

🅿

Hello,

Welcome to the third edition of this fantastic tool for self-discovery! The idea for this diary started in 2018, when I was studying at the Faculty of Astrological Studies in Oxford, England. I needed a quick guide to consult the positioning of the stars in the future but no such guide existed at the time. The following year, I independently published the first edition of *The Astrological Diary* in Brazil. It was much more successful than I had anticipated.

I guess one reason for this success is because people are increasingly seeking self-knowledge, wanting to learn how to manage their internal tools and become their own gurus.

With each edition I reinvent myself and discover and present a little of my studies to you. This year, 2023, is more than special, because the journal is becoming more and more like an astrological manual of natural magick, so that you can transform your life, using your own energy, following the music of the Universe.

Tarot, Kabbalah, Runes, rituals and sacred altars – all these things connect us with our own primordial essence, taking us back to a time when nature was our compass, when we could read more clearly the messages from the stars.

I hope I can help you reveal the light that exists inside you, that you can direct and command your life, using your own inner power in your favour, becoming the creator of your own destiny.

We are all cosmic dust, my beloveds,

Let's go together on this journey here on Earth,

Ana Leo

MY ASTRAL CHART

GO TO ASTRO.COM
AND MAKE YOUR FREE
CHART. COPY THE POSITION
OF EACH PLANET ONTO THIS
GRAPHIC. YOU'RE STARTING
TO GET IN TOUCH WITH
EVERY ASPECT OF YOUR
BIRTH CHART.

SOLAR & LUNAR CALENDARS

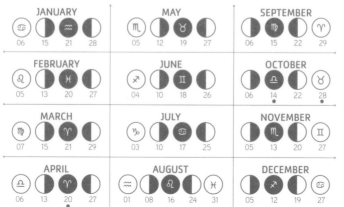

MOON PHASES
AND THE RIGHT ATTITUDE

NEW MOON
NEW BEGINNINGS
SET YOUR INTENTIONS
PLANT THE SEEDS
FOR THE NEXT 6 MONTHS

WAXING CRESCENT
BE CURIOUS
MOTIVATE
ATTRACT

FIRST QUARTER
TAKE ACTION
GROWTH
STRENGTH

WAXING GIBBOUS
IMPROVE
ALIGN YOUR DESIRES
REFINE PLANS

FULL MOON
CELEBRATION
HARVEST WHAT YOU PLANTED
6 MONTHS AGO

WANING GIBBOUS
SHARE
LOOK WITHIN
SAY THANKS

LAST QUARTER
RELEASE
LET GO OF BAD HABITS
CLEANSING

BALSAMIC MOON
SILENCE
MEDITATE
REST AND RELAX

SIGNS AND PLANETS

ARIES

TAURUS

GEMINI

CANCER

LEO

VIRGO

LIBRA

SCORPIO

SAGITTARIUS   CAPRICORN

AQUARIUS

PISCES

PERSONAL PLANETS

SUN

MOON

MERCURY

VENUS

MARS

SOCIAL AND TRANSPERSONAL PLANETS

JUPITER   SATURN   URANUS   NEPTUNE   PLUTO

PHASES OF THE MOON

| NEW MOON | WAXING CRESCENT | FIRST QUARTER | WAXING GIBBOUS | FULL MOON | WANING GIBBOUS | LAST QUARTER | WANING CRESCENT |

ELEMENTS

| FIRE | EARTH | AIR | WATER |

ASPECTS

| CONJUNCTION | SQUARE | SEXTILE | OPPOSITION | RETROGRADE | DIRECT | STATION |
| 0° | 90° | 60° | 180° | | | |

RETROGRADE PLANETS – 2023

MARS   **30/10/2022 – 12/01**   25º ♊ 8º ♊

MERCURY   **29/12/2022 – 18/01**   24º ♑ 8º ♑

URANUS   **24/08/2022 – 22/01**   18º ♉ 14º ♉

MERCURY   **21/04 – 15/05**   15º ♉ 5º ♉

PLUTO   **01/05 – 11/10**   0º ♒ 27º ♑

SATURN   **17/06 – 05/11**   7º ♓ 0º ♓

NEPTUNE   **30/06 – 07/12**   27º ♓ 24º ♓

VENUS   **22/07 – 04/09**   28º ♌ 12º ♌

MERCURY   **23/08 – 16/09**   21º ♍ 8º ♍

URANUS   **28/08 – 28/01/2024**   23º ♉ 19º ♉

JUPITER   **04/09 – 31/12**   15º ♉ 5º ♉

MERCURY   **13/12 – 03/01/2024**   8º ♑ 22º ♆

WHAT IS THE NEW MOON?

Every month the Sun and Moon meet in the sky. This meeting is undoubtedly the most powerful moment in the entire lunar cycle, as it contains the perfect energy to start a new chapter!

During the New Moon, the Sun and Moon are in the same mathematical degree in the Zodiac. Together they join forces to help us work for our intentions. It is this unity that creates a powerful vibration in the Universe and within each one of us. Our strength and emotion are bound together, as if an energetic and cosmic portal were opened and invited us to sow a seed of what we need to manifest in our lives. So, the New Moon is the perfect time to take a first step or start a project, because the energy of the Moon is so strong that we can direct it to make great energetic leaps in our lives.

At the Full Moon we observe our entire journey of the last six months. It is the culmination of the events that emerged on the New Moon. It is when the Sun is on the opposite side of the Moon, illuminating her conquests and opposing her energy. Use the two weeks after the New Moon to walk toward your goal and observe the first steps of your intentions. Work hand in hand with these cycles, so that in six months, when the Full Moon finally happens in that same sign, you will have a new reality manifested in your life.

The New Moon, besides giving us the opportunity to start something, also allows us an opening to balance our entire internal being, our soul, mind and spirit. Through the union of the Sun and the Moon, every month we have a new opportunity to create balance in our internal and external energies and consequently in our lives.

HOW TO MAKE THE MOST OF THIS MOMENT?

When the Sun and Moon are balanced, we are also balanced. Each month this diary will show you the ideal "theme" to work on, both in terms of your feelings and your actions.

The house on the Astral Chart where the New Moon takes place also gives us clues, showing us the area of our life where we must put all our intentions in motion.

The New Moon pages in this diary were created to guide you in the use of these energies and to help you identify the areas to be worked on. In some months you will be more motivated to act, in others you will be helped to vibrate what you want to feel.

Through the lens of the Zodiac, we are able to identify the right time to take action to transform our reality. The balance of these two vital energies is the key. When these two celestial bodies – the two most important luminaries for our daily life – come together in the sky to balance their energies, we must do the same!

HOW TO MANIFEST?
Rules to show your intentions to the Universe

The exact moment of the New Moon possesses the greatest energetic force, so it is a time when you can plant your intentions for the next cycle.

The twelve hours before this event are charged with this energy and must be used, both for introspection and for reflection. Six months separate a New Moon from a Full Moon, in the same sign.

This is the period when we see our desire grow. Following its development, it is the time to take care and give the necessary attention so that it manifests itself. Remember that your desire is like a seed that needs to be nourished every day so that it grows and bears flowers and fruit. Just creating the list and not taking any action to make it a reality will not take it off the paper.

Put at least five intentions on your list, always indicating what action is necessary for them to become reality. For example: I intend to lose 5kg – I will start walking three times a week. I intend to get a job – I will rewrite my resumé and send it to a specific company.

Make sure that you are asking a request from your soul, not your ego. The soul's desires require patience and dedication, and bring you long-term satisfaction. The ego's desires are superficial and only benefit you; your satisfaction is immediate and does not last for long.

Remember that you must feel as if you are already fulfilling all your wishes, so when you write them, imagine yourself as if they were already a reality. How would you feel? What would you say to other people? How would you describe it to the person who most wants to see your success? The greater the details in your imagination, the BETTER!

WHICH TIME ZONE IS CONSIDERED?
This diary can be used in all Northern Hemisphere countries

All the time zones with summertime adjustments are covered on the New Moon pages relative to UTC (Coordinated Universal Time). This year I have included the time zones of particular cities:

Los Angeles (UTC -8) • New York (UTC -5) • London (UTC +0)
Paris (UTC +1) • Sydney (UTC +10)

All the information in this diary has the intention to alert you before the aspect reaches its apex. European countries, as they are eight hours ahead of the Pacific, should consider the day as starting at 08:00 AM. So if the exact aspect perfection occurs at 03:00 AM CTU, the advice will be posted one day before. For most US readers, the day starts at 12:00 AM as usual. An aspect is always strongest as it builds, and then gradually weakens after it reaches its perfection (same degree and minute). Australian and Asian residents can prepare one day earlier. No matter where you are, with this diary, you will always be on time for the best energy to come!

THE TWELVE HOUSES OF THE HOROSCOPE

The following describes the general nature of each house:

I. FIRST HOUSE: Personality, natural disposition, worldly outlook generally. Physical experiences as obtained through the five senses. The parts of the body denoted are the head and face.

II. SECOND HOUSE: Finance, monetary prospects. Self-esteem values, salary, income. Desires caused by tenth house influence affecting moral growth. The parts of the body denoted are the throat and ears.

III. THIRD HOUSE: Relatives and kindred, travelling, intellect derived from education and study, first education, expression, and minor impressions made upon the physical brain. The parts of the body denoted are the neck, arms and shoulders and the lungs.

IV. FOURTH HOUSE: Hereditary tendencies, home and domestic life, parentage, ancestry, environment and the general state of things at the close of life. The parts of the body denoted are the breasts, stomach and digestive organs.

V. FIFTH HOUSE: Offspring, generative powers, sensations and pleasurable emotions arising from the senses, worldly enterprise and energy. Creativity and talents. The parts of the body denoted are the loins, heart and back.

VI. SIXTH HOUSE: Service and attachments arising from the expression of the tenth house, therefore servants and inferiors in social rank. This house also denotes sickness arising from worry and anxiety. It is also the house of phenomenal magick arising from everyday habits. The parts of the body denoted are the bowels and solar plexus.

VII. SEVENTH HOUSE: Unions, marriage, partnerships, business partner, spouse, individual character and humane tendencies, your client, your duo. The parts of the body denoted are the veins and kidneys.

VIII. EIGHTH HOUSE: Death, all matters pertaining to legacies or affairs connected with death. It is also what is termed an occult house, the womb, pregnancy, gestation. Fusion of energies, sexual drive. The parts of the body denoted are the secret parts and the generative system.

IX. NINTH HOUSE: Higher mentality, high studies, scientific, philosophical and religious tendencies. The searching of the path, your truth. It also denotes long journeys, documentation, certificates, dreams and the image-making power. The parts of the body denoted are the thighs and hips.

X. TENTH HOUSE: Profession, business ability, fame, honour and material reputation. All worldly activities and moral responsibilities are shown by this house, to succeed. The parts of the body denoted are the knees.

XI. ELEVENTH HOUSE: Friends, acquaintances, hopes, wishes and aspirations. The groups and environments you belong to. Your audience, your followers. The parts of the body denoted are the legs and ankles.

XII. TWELFTH HOUSE: Occult tendencies. Its connection with the fourth house shows the psychic thought inherited from the past and the result as either joy or sorrow. This may be said to be the most critical house of the twelve. The parts of the body denoted are the feet and toes.

LIFE SATISFACTION CHART

Each section represents an area of your life, or a house in your Astral Chart.
On a scale from 1 to 10, rate the areas of your chart.
You could use coloured pencils to make it artistic!

What could you do to increase your level of satisfaction in the areas with the lowest rates? Which area of your life, when you are satisfied, can increase all the other areas? Take time to think about it, and always come back to this page to track your progress!

EQUINOX

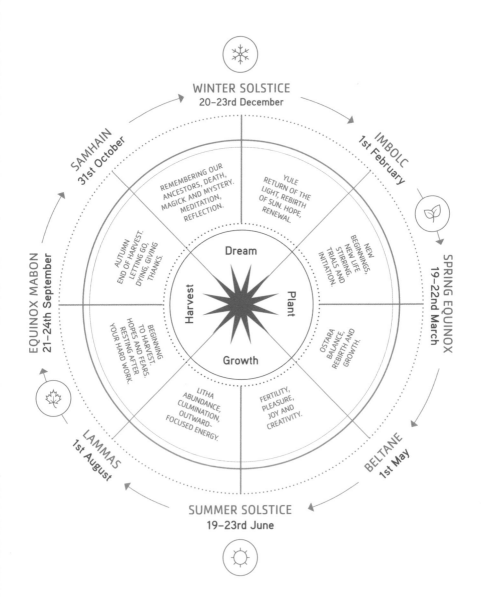

SACRED ALTAR

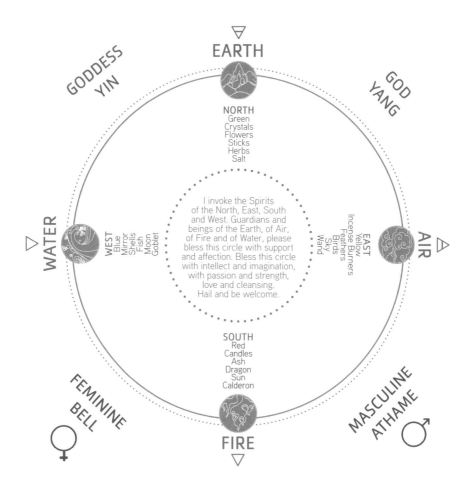

EARTH

GODDESS YIN

GOD YANG

NORTH
Green
Crystals
Flowers
Sticks
Herbs
Salt

WATER
Blue
Mirror
Shells
Fish
Moon
Goblet

WEST

I invoke the Spirits of the North, East, South and West. Guardians and beings of the Earth, of Air, of Fire and of Water, please bless this circle with support and affection. Bless this circle with intellect and imagination, with passion and strength, love and cleansing. Hail and be welcome.

EAST
Yellow
Incense Burners
Feathers
Birds
Sky
Wand

AIR

SOUTH
Red
Candles
Ash
Dragon
Sun
Calderon

FIRE

FEMININE BELL

MASCULINE ATHAME

A very simple ritual for creating a sacred space is to arrange the elements according to the cardinal directions, leaving the left side with Yin energy, while the right side carries the Yang polarity. Invoke the guardian elements to help you create your own magick. When you have finished your ritual, remember to close the circle, thanking the spirits and saying goodbye to them.

TAROT & ASTROLOGY
Major Arcana Correspondence

0. THE FOOL		AIR / URANUS	New beginnings, wonder, innocence, foolishness
1. THE MAGICIAN		MERCURY	Mastery, creation, willpower, manifestation
2. THE HIGH PRIESTESS		MOON	Intuition, divine wisdom, inner voice
3. THE EMPRESS		VENUS	Creativity, beauty, nurturing, fertility
4. THE EMPEROR		ARIES	Authority, ambition, fostering discipline
5. THE HIEROPHANT		TAURUS	Tradition, convention, spiritual wisdom
6. THE LOVERS		GEMINI	Love, union, relationship choices
7. THE CHARIOT		CANCER	Discipline, self-control, success
8. STRENGTH		LEO	Courage, inner strength, compassion
9. THE HERMIT		VIRGO	Insight, awareness, solitude, contemplation
10. WHEEL OF FORTUNE		JUPITER	Destiny, karma, fate, fortune

11. JUSTICE		LIBRA	Truth, law, fairness, clarity, cause and effect
12. THE HANGED MAN		WATER / NEPTUNE	Sacrifice, release, new perspective
13. DEATH		SCORPIO	Change, transformation, end of cycle
14. TEMPERANCE		SAGITTARIUS	Patience, finding meaning, balance
15. THE DEVIL		CAPRICORN	Materialism, pleasure, obsession, addiction
16. THE TOWER		MARS	Foundational shift, upheaval, drastic change
17. THE STAR		AQUARIUS	Faith, hope, healing, rejuvenation
18. THE MOON		PISCES	Intuition, unconsciousness, illusions
19. THE SUN		SUN	Joy, success, pleasure, celebration
20. JUDGEMENT		FIRE / PLUTO	Reflection, awakening, reckoning
21. THE WORLD		EARTH / SATURN	Completion, peace, fulfilment, harmony

A SPELL FOR EACH TIME AND EACH SIGN!

Combine the Energy of Your Sign or the Sign in Transit at Every Moment to Improve Your Magickal Abilities Even More!

♈ **Fire Witch –** focuses on the five element, does a lot of work involving candles, burning, etc.

♉ **Green Witch –** based on the use of herbs and plants in magick, very natural and earth-based.

♊ **Crystal Witch –** works with stones, crystals, gemstones, for healing and other spells, deals with chakras.

♋ **Kitchen Witch –** uses magick incorporated with cooking and baking. Can conjure items for spell or ritual use.

♌ **Lunar Witch –** attunes to/honours the Moon cycles and phases. Likes to wake at night under the Moon energy.

♍ **Forest Witch –** works best surrounded by trees, is familiar with local plants and animals and herbal healing.

♎ **Music Witch –** magick is deeply rooted in music, has certain connection with sound and uses that to enhance rituals.

♏ **Nocturnal Witch –** embraces darker energies. Likes night-time and its mysteries. Works mostly after midnight.

♐ **Storm Witch –** combines its energy with that of the weather. Collects elements such as rainwater, leaves and rocks for spells.

♑ **Astronomy Witch –** all its magick aligns with stars and planets, practises astrology and recognizes placements and their significances.

♒ **Divination Witch –** works with various forms of divination, such as Tarot reading, palmistry, tea leaves, geomancy.

♓ **Sea Witch –** uses oceans and their magick practices, utilizing the natural objects in the sea such as salt water, shells, driftwood, etc.

2023

JANUARY

M	T	W	T	F	S	S
						1
2	3	4	5	6	7	8
9	10	11	12	13	14	15
16	17	18	19	20	21	22
23	24	25	26	27	28	29
30	31					

FEBRUARY

M	T	W	T	F	S	S
		1	2	3	4	5
6	7	8	9	10	11	12
13	14	15	16	17	18	19
20	21	22	23	24	25	26
27	28					

MARCH

M	T	W	T	F	S	S
		1	2	3	4	5
6	7	8	9	10	11	12
13	14	15	16	17	18	19
20	21	22	23	24	25	26
27	28	29	30	31		

APRIL

M	T	W	T	F	S	S
					1	2
3	4	5	6	7	8	9
10	11	12	13	14	15	16
17	18	19	20	21	22	23
24	25	26	27	28	29	30

MAY

M	T	W	T	F	S	S
1	2	3	4	5	6	7
8	9	10	11	12	13	14
15	16	17	18	19	20	21
22	23	24	25	26	27	28
29	30	31				

JUNE

M	T	W	T	F	S	S
			1	2	3	4
5	6	7	8	9	10	11
12	13	14	15	16	17	18
19	20	21	22	23	24	25
26	27	28	29	30		

JULY

M	T	W	T	F	S	S
					1	2
3	4	5	6	7	8	9
10	11	12	13	14	15	16
17	18	19	20	21	22	23
24	25	26	27	28	29	30
31						

AUGUST

M	T	W	T	F	S	S
	1	2	3	4	5	6
7	8	9	10	11	12	13
14	15	16	17	18	19	20
21	22	23	24	25	26	27
28	29	30	31			

SEPTEMBER

M	T	W	T	F	S	S
				1	2	3
4	5	6	7	8	9	10
11	12	13	14	15	16	17
18	19	20	21	22	23	24
25	26	27	28	29	30	

OCTOBER

M	T	W	T	F	S	S
						1
2	3	4	5	6	7	8
9	10	11	12	13	14	15
16	17	18	19	20	21	22
23	24	25	26	27	28	29
30	31					

NOVEMBER

M	T	W	T	F	S	S
		1	2	3	4	5
6	7	8	9	10	11	12
13	14	15	16	17	18	19
20	21	22	23	24	25	26
27	28	29	30			

DECEMBER

M	T	W	T	F	S	S
				1	2	3
4	5	6	7	8	9	10
11	12	13	14	15	16	17
18	19	20	21	22	23	24
25	26	27	28	29	30	31

01 JAN	New Year's Day
16 JAN	Martin Luther King Jr Day (US)
01 FEB	Chinese New Year
14 FEB	Valentine's Day
21 FEB	Shrove Tuesday
08 MAR	Internatiohnal Women's Day
17 MAR	St Patrick's Day
19 MAR	Mother's Day (UK)
20 MAR	Spring Equinox
07 APR	Good Friday
09 APR	Easter
10 APR	Easter Monday
01 MAY	Early May Bank Holiday (UK)
14 MAY	Mother's Day (US)
29 MAY	Memorial Day (US)
29 MAY	Spring Bank Holiday (UK)
18 JUN	Father's Day
21 JUN	Summer Solstice
04 JUL	Independence Day (US)
28 AUG	Summer Bank Holiday (UK)
04 SEP	Labor Day (US)
23 SEP	Autumn Equinox
31 OCT	Halloween
23 NOV	Thanksgiving (US)
22 DEC	Winter Solstice
25 DEC	Christmas Day
31 DEC	New Year's Eve

JANUARY

the first day
of the month
starts with the
ephemeris

☉ 10º ♑

☽ 9º ♉

☿ᴿ 24º ♑

♀ 28º ♑

♂ᴿ 9º ♊

♃ 1º ♈

♄ 22º ♒

♅ᴿ 15º ♉

♆ 23º ♓

♇ 28º ♑

MON	TUE	WED
02	03	04
09	10	11
16	17	18
23	24	25
30	31	

THU	FRI	SAT	SUN
			01
05	06	07	08
12	13	14	15
19	20	21	22
26	27	28	29

DEC
31
SAT

 ✩

JAN
01
SUN

♀ ☌ ♇ ♑
Venus meets Pluto in Capricorn

The year has barely begun and the Goddess Venus, who
rules the feminine energy, meets Pluto, lord of the depths
and of hidden treasures. This year already promises a
feminine revolution in business and finance. Do you already
know what you want to achieve in 2023? A great moment
to make your powerful wish list!

☽ ♉
Moon in Taurus

S M T W T F S S M T W T F S S M T W T F S S M T W T F S S M T
1 2 3 4 5 6 **7 8** 9 10 11 12 13 **14 15** 16 17 18 19 20 **21 22** 23 24 25 26 27 **28 29** 30 31

☿ ℞ ♑ ✳ ♆ ♓
Mercury Rx in Capricorn sextile Neptune in Pisces

JAN
02
MON

Mercury Rx wants to insist on a dream that is impossible, or difficult to build. When it meets Neptune, it is time to dream of what can be built. Leave illusions aside and beware of misunderstandings. Today our mind is flying high, excellent for great insights.

♀ ♒
Venus enters Aquarius until 26th January

After the encounter with Pluto, Venus wants nothing less than a collective desire. She wants to impact more and more people, so it's a great time to reflect whether your wishes involve other people or only benefit yourself. A friendship can become romance or vice versa. Our concept of free love gains amplitude and we just need to be attentive that we are managing to externalize our emotions in the right way.

☽ ♊
Moon in Gemini

JAN
03
TUE

☽ ♊
Moon in Gemini

JAN
04
WED

♀ ≈ ✳ ♃ ♈
Venus in Aquarius sextile Jupiter in Aries

Wednesday is excellent for promoting a competition or doing something fun and lively as a group. Leading a team, calling friends for board games, and any mental or physical exercise that encourages healthy competition is welcome. Taking part in a poll on social networks with prizes would be a great idea.

☽ ♊
Moon in Gemini

JAN
05
THU

☉ ♑ △ ♅ ♉
Sun in Capricorn trine Uranus Rx in Taurus

It is likely that you will feel the need to be valued among friends. Or it may be that you have been wanting to change some equipment or invest in some powerful machinery for your business. Do the maths and wait for Uranus to return to direct motion before you make new purchases.

☽ ♋
Moon in Cancer

JAN
06
FRI

○ ♋
Full Moon 16º Cancer

✩

JAN
07
SAT

☉ ☌ ☿ ℞ ♑
Sun meets Mercury Rx in Capricorn

When the Sun and Mercury Rx meet it is because we are
halfway to a new mental upgrade. An excellent time to
review everything that has gone on in the last ten days, and
continue reviewing and revising all documents, papers and
anything that requires our signature and decision. Soon
Mercury will give us the green light again.

☽ ♌
Moon in Leo

JAN
08
SUN

☿ ℞ ♑ △ ♅ ℞ ♉
Mercury Rx in Capricorn trine
Uranus Rx in Taurus

A regret may arise about something
commented on by you on social networks,
a post that did not go down very well with
your audience, something that needs to be
rethought and reformulated. A great time
to take a look at your profiles and start an
update of your virtual persona.

☽ ♌
Moon in Leo

JAN
09
MON

♀ ♒ △ ♂ ℞ ♊
Venus in Aquarius trine Mars Rx in Gemini

A conversation that was previously put aside may be
revisited, some argument or misunderstanding with friends
or partners may ask for your opinion again. Since you are a
little detached, make sure you don't throw everything away
for good. We can love many people at the same time, but
everyone should know exactly what your intentions are.
Put your cards on the table!

☽ ♌
Moon in Leo

S M T W T F S S M T W T F S S M T W T F S S M T W T F S S M T
1 2 3 4 5 6 7 8 9 10 11 12 13 **14 15** 16 17 18 19 20 **21 22** 23 24 25 26 27 **28 29** 30 31

JAN
10
TUE

☽ ♍
Moon in Virgo

JAN
11
WED

☽ ♍
Moon in Virgo

JAN
12
THU

♂ St D ♊
Mars St Direct 8º in Gemini

Finally, after four months, Mars – which rules our
actions and impulses – says goodbye to the retrograde
movement where he learned to communicate in
another way, perhaps not so impulsive and sarcastic.
Time to work for all those ideals he talks about so
much. Tomorrow everything is back on track again!

☽ ♎
Moon in Libra

JAN
13
FRI

☉ ♑ ⚹ Ψ ♓
Sun in Capricorn sextile Neptune in Pisces

A Friday to celebrate your achievements. If you
have a big dream and you know how to make it
come true, you have already given it structure
and are looking for financial resources, this
is a good time to dream in public. Make your
presentation to those who you think will invest
in your project. Good luck!

♂ D ♊
Mars Direct 8º in Gemini

Green light to defend all your ideas without
offending or disrespecting others. We have
learned this lesson well, never to repeat it
again. Put your ideas into practice now!

☽ ♎
Moon in Libra

JAN
14
SAT

◑ ♎︎
Last Quarter 24º Libra

Saturday is a little melancholy. Relationships lose some
strength of passion with this waning Moon in Libra. Fill
your gaze with beautiful things, read poetry, listen to
classical music and let go of everything you no longer like.

JAN
15
SUN

♀ ♒︎ □ ♅ ℞ ♉︎
Venus in Aquarius squares Uranus Rx in Taurus

Venus wants to win the world and you want to be
a leader in social networks. You want to command
social reform, but we are not always received
the way we expect. Your idealism can easily be
frustrated by others – don't let it get you down.

☽ ♏︎
Moon in Scorpio

JAN
16
MON

☽ ♏
Moon in Scorpio

JAN
17
TUE

☽ ♐
Moon in Sagittarius

☿ St D ♑
Mercury St Direct in 8º Capricorn

JAN
18
WED

We have had 20 days of mental reprogramming, to review our plans and deadlines, how we are building our future, and now we are more prepared than ever. Starting tomorrow, we can commit to everything that was waiting for our response.

☉ ♂ ♇ ♑
Sun meets Pluto in Capricorn

It is a very revealing aspect: situations that were previously under the protection of darkness and ignorance tend to come to light. Things we suspected were not going well may be confirmed that they are truly not going well. To begin something it is necessary to finish what we have already started.

☽ ♐
Moon in Sagittarius

JAN
19
THU

☿ D ♑
Mercury Direct in Capricorn

Your power of persuasion gains strength and you can now convince whoever you want of your plans and projects. An excellent time to be recognized for an idea, to present your research or to be accepted in a much better position than previously.

☽ ♑
Moon in Capricorn

JAN
20
FRI

⊙ ♒︎
Sun enters Aquarius

The Sun enters the independent and unconventional sign
of Aquarius and we all gain some of that energy. Maximum
concentration, patience with progress, determination –
these are some of the characteristics we now count on in
our journey. Time to see ourselves as part of all humanity!

☽ ♑︎
Moon in Capricorn

JAN
21
SAT

● ♒︎
New Moon 1º Aquarius

In time for the New Moon in Aquarius, your ruler Uranus
begins the awakening to a New Age. Time to plant the
seeds in the collective, decide which group of friends you
want to lead, what revolution you propose to yourself for
this year. Write everything down on the New Moon page.

S M T W T F S S M T W T F S S M T W T F S S M T W T F S S M T
1 2 3 4 5 6 7 8 9 10 11 12 13 14 15 16 17 18 19 20 21 22 23 24 25 26 27 28 29 30 31

AQUARIUS

January 20th / 08:29am (UTC)

AIR

URANUS

AQUARIUS

MODE Fixed   **ELEMENT** Air   **RULING PLANET** Uranus

CRYSTAL Cornelian   **BACH FLOWER REMEDY** Water Violet

PRINCIPLE Positive   **OPPOSITE SIGN** Leo

AQUARIUS AND SIGNS IN LOVE

Aries	♥ ♥ ♥ ♡ ♡	Libra	♥ ♥ ♥ ♥ ♥
Taurus	♥ ♡ ♡ ♡ ♡	Scorpio	♥ ♥ ♡ ♡ ♡
Gemini	♥ ♥ ♥ ♥ ♥	Sagittarius	♥ ♥ ♥ ♥ ♡
Cancer	♥ ♥ ♡ ♡ ♡	Capricorn	♥ ♥ ♡ ♡ ♡
Leo	♥ ♥ ♥ ♥ ♥	Aquarius	♥ ♥ ♥ ♡ ♡
Virgo	♥ ♥ ♡ ♡ ♡	Pisces	♥ ♥ ♡ ♡ ♡

MANTRA I know   **POWER** Vision

KEYWORD Imagination   **ANATOMY** Ankles

LIGHT	SHADOW
Independent	Unpredictable
Inventive	Temperamental
Individualistic	Bored with details
Progressive	Cold
Artistic	Too fixed opinions
Logical	Shy
Eccentric	Radical
Intellectual	Impersonal
Altruistic	Rebellious

Meditation for the month of Sh'vat
Scan with your eyes from right to left

A Q U A R I U S

JANUARY 21ST – 8:53PM (UTC) – 1° AQUARIUS

Los Angeles (UTC -8) • New York (UTC -5) • London (UTC +0)
Paris (UTC +1) • Sydney (UTC +11)

SET YOUR INTENTIONS FOR THE NEXT 6 MONTHS

_____

_____

_____

_____

_____

HOW ARE YOU GOING TO GET THERE?

_____

_____

_____

_____

_____

New friendships	Futurist	Detachment
Collective	Internet and social	Leaving addictions
New projects	networks	Originality
Innovation	Eccentricity	Activism

JAN
22
SUN

♀ ♂ ♄ ♒
Venus meets Saturn in Aquarius

Not a very delicate Sunday, as Venus is not comfortable in the austere presence of Saturn. You may feel greedier than usual, but not in a good way. You may be irritated by the tactlessness of human beings, or the perverse side of humanity. Take a deep breath: it's just a not very nice day.

♅ St D ♉
Uranus St Direct 14º in Taurus

After five months in retrograde mode, Uranus begins its awakening and all technologies, media and magnetic waves gain strength from tomorrow. Watch out for electronics that may pick up this vibration and go off for a few moments.

JAN
23
MON

♅ D ♉
Uranus Direct in Taurus

Monday starts with the radius of Uranus determining that it's time to revolutionize another cycle of life. We have seven months of technological advance ahead of us. Have you already created your digital plan for 2023? This is the time!

☽ ♓
Moon in Pisces

S M T W T F S S M T W T F S S M T W T F S S M T W T F S S M T
1 2 3 4 5 6 7 8 9 10 11 12 13 **14 15** 16 17 18 19 20 **21 22** 23 24 25 26 27 **28 29** 30 31

JAN

24

TUE

☉ ♒ ✳ ♃ ♈
Sun in Aquarius sextile
Jupiter in Aries

Wonderful aspect to amplify our
horizons and celebrate our collective
victories as a group. Cultural festivals,
public celebrations, music concerts,
sports – everything that is intended
today gains strong social popularity.

☽ ♓
Moon in Pisces

JAN

25

WED

☽ ♈
Moon in Aries

JAN
26
THU

♀ ♓
Venus enters Pisces until 20th February

Venus in Pisces means immensity of emotions. It amplifies our natural side of love and compassion, intensifying beauty, which can be expressed through music, poetry, painting or any form of art and grace. Resources can come through helping others or donating. A great time for both of these activities. Enjoy!

☽ ♈
Moon in Aries

JAN
27
FRI

☽ ♉
Moon in Taurus

JAN
28
SAT

◗ ♉
First Quarter 8° Taurus

Excellent time to set your financial
intentions for this year. Are you receiving
the resources you need to feel secure and
comfortable? If so, set a higher goal to
be met by the Full Moon which will be a
Partial Eclipse at the end of October.

JAN
29
SUN

☉ ♒ △ ♂ ♊
Sun in Aquarius trine Mars in Gemini

Although it's Sunday, it's a good day to put
all your most ambitious plans into action.
How can you take the first step to turn a
great idea into something tangible? Today
is the day when your plans can start to
take real shape – invest in them!

☽ ♉
Moon in Taurus

JAN
30
MON

☽ ♊
Moon in Gemini

JAN
31
TUE

☽ ♊
Moon in Gemini

FEBRUARY

the first day
of the month
starts with the
ephemeris

☉ 12º ♒

☽ 25º ♊

☿ 17º ♑

♀ 6º ♓

♂ 10º ♊

♃ 6º ♈

♄ 25º ♒

♅ 14º ♉

♆ 23º ♓

♇ 28º ♑

MON	TUE	WED
		01
06	07	08
13	14	15
20	21	22
27	28	

THU	FRI	SAT	SUN
02	03	04	05
09	10	11	12
16	17	18	19
23	24	25	26

FEB

01

WED

☽ ♋
Moon in Cancer

FEB

02

THU

☽ ♋
Moon in Cancer

W T F S S M T W T F S S M T W T F S S M T W T F S S M T
1 2 3 **4** 5 6 7 8 9 10 **11** **12** 13 14 15 16 17 **18** **19** 20 21 22 23 24 **25** **26** 27 28

FEB
03
FRI

☉ ♒ □ ♅ ♉
Sun in Aquarius square Uranus in Taurus

A tense aspect in the sky could indicate
devaluation of a group of people through
networking. Beware of the generalized
opinions you expose, and don't make
any big technological moves today.

☽ ♋
Moon in Cancer

FEB
04
SAT

♀ ♓ □ ♂ ♊
Venus in Pisces squares Mars in Gemini

Venus wants depth and total, unconditional
surrender, but Mars still has many doubts,
wants to test other paths and acts more
superficially. It is not a good day to talk with
your partner. Avoid falling into this polarity!

☽ ♌
Moon in Leo

FEB
05
SUN

○ ♌
Full Moon 16º Leo

FEB
06
MON

☿ ♑ ⚹ ♆ ♓
Mercury in Capricorn sextile
Neptune in Pisces

After the tension in relationships at
the weekend, this aspect helps us to
talk about our dreams for the future.
A good day to align expectations
with your partner or business
partner. Good for presentations
and important meetings.

☽ ♍
Moon in Virgo

W T F S S M T W T F S S M T W T F S S M T W T F S S M T
1 2 3 4 5 6 7 8 9 10 11 12 13 14 15 16 17 18 19 20 21 22 23 24 25 26 27 28

FEB
07
TUE

☽ ♍
Moon in Virgo

FEB
08
WED

♀ ♓ ✳ ♅ ♉
Venus in Pisces sextile
Uranus in Taurus

A special transit to receive a loving
surprise. You could receive a message
from someone special, or a bouquet of
flowers. Watch for all demonstrations
of care and affection today.

☽ ♍
Moon in Virgo

W T F S S M T W T F S S M T W T F S S M T W T F S S M T
1 2 3 4 5 6 7 8 9 10 11 12 13 14 15 16 17 18 19 20 21 22 23 24 25 26 27 28

FEB
09
THU

☽ ♎
Moon in Libra

FEB
10
FRI

☿ ☌ ♇ ♑
Mercury meets Pluto in Capricorn

A powerful Friday for talking to important
people. Perfect day to have a meeting
with your superiors or someone who
has more power than you but can help
you on your way to success. Share your
treasures and you will be rewarded!

☽ ♎
Moon in Libra

FEB

11

SAT

☿ ♒
Mercury enters Aquarius
until 2nd March

After the meeting with Pluto, Mercury
now gains agility and only thinks about
future plans. Begin structuring and
planning everything you intended at
the New Moon in Aquarius. Move
forward with the plans and in life!

☽ ♏
Moon in Scorpio

FEB

12

SUN

☽ ♏
Moon in Scorpio

FEB
13
MON

◗ ♎
Last Quarter 24º Scorpio

Make a spa at home, prepare
a bath of salts, an exfoliation
– free yourself from old skin,
and prepare for a renewed
week of love and hope.

FEB
14
TUE

☽ ♐
Moon in Sagittarius

W T F S S M T W T F S S M T W T F S S M T W T F S S M T
1 2 3 4 5 6 7 8 9 10 11 12 13 14 15 16 17 18 19 20 21 22 23 24 25 26 27 28

FEB

15

WED

♀ ☌ ♆ ♓
Venus meets Neptune in Pisces

The most romantic day of the year is when
Venus and Neptune meet in the depths of
the sea of love. A day to share what you
are best at, your passionate views and
caring outlook on people. Celebrate self-
love by also really spoiling yourself.

☽ ♐
Moon in Sagittarius

FEB

16

THU

☉ ☌ ♄ ♒
Sun meets Saturn in Aquarius

After the shower of love comes the shock
of reality! The Sun and Saturn are in a
stiff conversation regarding how we can
be better on a societal level. Are you
committed to making the planet a better
place? Saturn is demanding answers.

☽ ♑
Moon in Capricorn

FEB
17
FRI

☿ ♒ ✳ ♃ ♈
Mercury in Aquarius sextile Jupiter in Aries

All the structuring proposed by Mercury now
gains much greater amplitude by joining with
Jupiter, which wants to take risks and enforce
this new plan for success. Get together with
other people who are interested in taking risks
with you, so that you can form a dream team!

☽ ♑
Moon in Capricorn

FEB
18
SAT

☉ ♓
Sun enters Pisces

The most enchanted month of the year has just
begun and we want to throw ourselves into the sea
of emotions of Pisces. Great for all subjects related
to arts, culture, video, photography and everything
you are passionate about, putting your heart to the
fore. This year with Jupiter we will have an explosion
of these themes for sure! Enjoy and have fun!

☽ ♒
Moon in Aquarius

PISCES

February 18th / 10:34pm (UTC)

WATER

NEPTUNE

PISCES

MODE Mutable   **ELEMENT** Water   **RULING PLANET** Neptune

CRYSTAL Amethyst   **BACH FLOWER REMEDY** Rock Rose

PRINCIPLE Negative   **OPPOSITE SIGN** Virgo

PISCES AND SIGNS IN LOVE

Aries	♥ ♥ ♥ ♡ ♡	Libra	♥ ♥ ♡ ♡ ♡
Taurus	♥ ♥ ♥ ♥ ♡	Scorpio	♥ ♥ ♥ ♥ ♥
Gemini	♥ ♡ ♡ ♡ ♡	Sagittarius	♥ ♥ ♥ ♥ ♡
Cancer	♥ ♥ ♥ ♡ ♡	Capricorn	♥ ♥ ♥ ♡ ♡
Leo	♥ ♥ ♥ ♥ ♡	Aquarius	♥ ♥ ♡ ♡ ♡
Virgo	♥ ♥ ♥ ♥ ♥	Pisces	♥ ♥ ♥ ♥ ♥

MANTRA I Believe   **POWER** Comprehension

KEYWORD Intuition   **ANATOMY** Feet

LIGHT	SHADOW
Compassionate	Procrastinator
Charitable	Very talkative
Friendly	Melancholic
Emotional	Pessimistic
Makes sacrifices	Emotionally inhibited
Intuitive	Shy
Introspective	Impractical
Musical	Indolent
Artistic	Often feels misunderstood

Meditation for the month of Adar
Scan with your eyes from right to left

P I S C E S

FEBRUARY 20TH – 7:06AM (UTC) – 1° PISCES

Los Angeles (UTC -8) • New York (UTC -5) • London (UTC +0)
Paris (UTC +1) • Sydney (UTC +11)

SET YOUR INTENTIONS FOR THE NEXT 6 MONTHS

_____

_____

_____

_____

_____

HOW ARE YOU GOING TO GET THERE?

_____

_____

_____

_____

_____

Inspiration	Transcendence	Intuition
Unconditional love	Compassion	Altruism
Be enlightened	Spirituality	Philanthropy
Mysticism	Collective unconscious	Charity

FEB
19
SUN

♀ ♓ ✳ ♇ ♑
Venus in Pisces sextile
Pluto in Capricorn

Venus wants unconditional love but also desires
recognition for all your self-giving in recent times.
If you are looking for humanitarian causes to fulfil
yourself as a human being, today is the best day
to shine and spread your light. Love is truly the
most powerful force in the Universe – believe it!

☽ ♒
Moon in Aquarius

FEB
20
MON

♀ ♈
Venus enters Aries until 16th March

After lessons of self-love and giving, Venus
is ready to get bolder and risk a little more in
the strategy of conquest. In Aries, passions
tend to be ephemeral and fleeting. Don't play
with fire if you don't want to get burned!

● ♓
New Moon 1º Pisces

The New Moon in Pisces asks us to plant our
seeds in unconditional love. Mysticism is in the
air; we are more psychic than ever. Stop for a
moment, close your eyes and receive some divine
insights. How can you contribute to a world with
fewer emotional barriers? Think about it.

FEB
21
TUE

☿ ♒ □ ♅ ♉
Mercury in Aquarius squares Uranus in Taurus

Difficulty in being able to expose your great
ideals virtually. It is time for you to decide the
strategy of how to spread your message using
social networks. It will be a big challenge to
translate all your thoughts into html codes, but
with the right people, success is guaranteed.

☽ ♓
Moon in Pisces

FEB
22
WED

☿ ♒ △ ♂ ♊
Mercury in Aquarius trine Mars in Gemini

It may be that destiny brings you the right
challenge at the right time, so that you
understand who you can count on to help
you spread that message. Diversify and try to
find a more light-hearted partnership. Maybe
someone younger could help you better.

☽ ♈
Moon in Aries

FEB
23
THU

☽ ♈
Moon in Aries

FEB
24
FRI

☽ ♉
Moon in Taurus

FEB
25
SAT

☽ ♉
Moon in Taurus

FEB
26
SUN

☽ ♊
Moon in Gemini

W T F S S M T W T F S S M T W T F S S M T W T F S S M T
1 2 3 4 5 6 7 8 9 10 11 12 13 14 15 16 17 18 19 20 21 22 23 24 25 26 27 28

FEB
27
MON

◐ ♊
First Quarter 8º Gemini

Use Monday to grow your network, a good
day to look for the right people to help you
manifest your dreams. Also an excellent time
for you to activate that important person you
met by chance at some event. Grow and
strengthen your ties with the right people!

FEB
28
TUE

☽ ♋
Moon in Cancer

MARCH

the first day
of the month
starts with the
ephemeris

☉	10º	♓
☽	4º	♋
☿	27º	♒
♀	11º	♈
♂	19º	♊
♃	12º	♈
♄	29º	♒
♅	15º	♉
♆	24º	♓
♇	29º	♑

MON	TUE	WED
		01
06	07	08
13	14	15
20	21	22
27	28	29

THU	FRI	SAT	SUN
02	03	04	05
09	10	11	12
16	17	18	19
23	24	25	26
30	31		

MAR
01
WED

☽ ♋
Moon in Cancer

♀ ☌ ♃ ♈
Venus meets Jupiter in Aries

MAR
02
THU

Day full of aspects! Starting with Venus amplifying your fire and magnetism with the presence of Jupiter, it will be difficult not to show your desire. We are easily attracted to the unknown, and Jupiter encourages this jumping into the abyss! Popularity is at 1,000 per cent – today you'll win all the attention you desire!

☿ ☌ ♄ ♒
Mercury meets Saturn in Aquarius

While Venus attracts the spotlight, Mercury pulls you toward commitment to the collective. Saturn wants your ideals well structured, however, so we have a bit of everything. Take responsibility before jumping into the creative side.

☿ ♓
Mercury enters Pisces until 19th March

At the end of the day Mercury loses a little focus and now only thinks about creating something beautiful and new to be admired by the public. Artistic presentations are in full swing today!

☽ ♋
Moon in Cancer

MAR
03
FRI

☽ ♌
Moon in Leo

MAR
04
SAT

☽ ♌
Moon in Leo

MAR
05
SUN

☽ ♌
Moon in Leo

MAR
06
MON

☉ ♓ ✳ ♅ ♉
Sun in Pisces sextile Uranus in Taurus

Expose your talents virtually once again.
Any action to make you even more
heard, seen and noticed virtually has a
great chance of working. Promote your
profiles, your website, your LinkedIn.

☽ ♍
Moon in Virgo

MAR
07
TUE

♄ ♓
Saturn enters Pisces until 25th March 2025

After more than two years of transiting through Aquarius, Saturn enters in Pisces to bring even more structure to our dreams and to make us commit to daily actions of donation and compassion for our fellows. We have two years to embrace the pain of the world, and help to heal it!

○ ♍
Full Moon 16º Virgo

On the same day, the Full Moon is pushing us into service for what needs to be done! Excellent combination for all who work with the less fortunate, or in the medical field. On the individual level, it is time to look at your health and your work routine.

MAR
08
WED

☽ ♎
Moon in Libra

MAR

09

THU

☽ ♎
Moon in Libra

MAR

10

FRI

☽ ♏
Moon in Scorpio

MAR
11
SAT

♀ ♈ ✳ ♂ ♊
Venus in Aries sextile
Mars in Gemini

Wonderful Saturday for going out,
meeting new people and perhaps
falling in love again. Venus is flirting
and Mars wants a taste of that
passion. Socialize and have fun!

☿ ♓ ✳ ♅ ♉
Mercury in Pisces sextile
Uranus in Taurus

Good for virtual presentations,
music concerts or cinema. It's a
very creative weekend – explore
your talents alone or in a group.

☽ ♏
Moon in Scorpio

MAR
12
SUN

☽ ♏
Moon in Scorpio

MAR
13
MON

☽ ♐
Moon in Sagittarius

MAR
14
TUE

♂ ♊ ◻ ♆ ♓
Mars in Gemini squares Neptune in Pisces

Not a good day for making big decisions
or rethinking attitudes. Your attention
is not fully focused so don't expect too
much from yourself or others. Good for
all artistic and or solitary activities.

◑ ♐
Last Quarter 24º Sagittarius

We leave a truth behind, a philosophy of
life that no longer fits our personality;
something we have pursued for a long time
loses strength. Just let go and surrender.

MAR
15
WED

☉ ♂ ♆ ♓
Sun meets Neptune in Pisces

The most dispersed day of the year, excellent if
you practise painting, sculpture or any other kind of
active meditation or artistic activity, but a bad day for
anything that requires your concentration or attention.
Wait until next week for that important meeting.

☽ ♑
Moon in Capricorn

☿ ♂ ♆ ♓
Mercury meets Neptune in Pisces

Another day of excitement within and in the Cosmos, but don't
rush into anything on impulse. Our rational communication has
a distorted filter. The word is Silver but the silence is Gold.

MAR
16
THU

☉ ♓ □ ♂ ♊
Sun in Pisces squares Mars in Gemini

There are so many options, so many doubts, the
perfect place for a big anxiety crisis. Try to breathe
and don't cling to any intrusive thoughts today.

♀ ♈ □ ♇ ♑
Venus in Aries squares Pluto in Capricorn

Venus wants and wants it all now! This conversation with Pluto
couldn't come at a worse time. Wait for the dust to settle, she'll be
back home soon and things will be a little more stable. Patience!

♀ ♉
Venus enters Taurus until 11th April

In her house everything is more comfortable: Venus can take off that heavy armour
and put on her silk dress, take off her high heels and walk with her feet on the
ground. Unload all the energy of the last days by walking barefoot on the grass!

MAR

17

FRI

☿ ♓ □ ♂ ♊
Mercury in Pisces squares Mars in Gemini

Still in the loose motion of this whole week, today's aspects are only favourable for creation, for the arts, music, something improvised and a little crazy. Other than that, all other activities are compromised by lack of focus!

☉ ♂ ☿ ♓
Sun meets Mercury in Pisces

The Sun in Pisces, super mystical, gains a beautiful messenger to help you spread your message of love throughout the world. All spiritual practices are welcome as it is time to listen to the heart.

♀ ♉ ✳ ♄ ♓
Venus in Taurus sextile Saturn in Pisces

In the midst of so much dispersion, Venus thinks about how she can feel even more valued by helping her fellow humans. Create a plan, or find a charity that you can help. You'll feel great about it!

☽ ♒
Moon in Aquarius

MAR

18

SAT

☿ ♓ ✳ ♇ ♑
Mercury in Pisces sextile Pluto in Capricorn

Another powerful Saturday for all things cultural. We are well committed to our mission of helping the planet. Have an important conversation with someone who means a lot to you. Align your goals together!

☽ ♒
Moon in Aquarius

ARIES

March 20th / 9:24pm (UTC)

△

FIRE

♂

MARS

ARIES

MODE Cardinal   **ELEMENT** Fire   **RULING PLANET** Mars

CRYSTAL Pyrite   **BACH FLOWER REMEDY** Impatiens

PRINCIPLE Positive   **OPPOSITE SIGN** Libra

ARIES AND SIGNS IN LOVE

Aries	♥ ♥ ♥ ♡ ♡	Libra	♥ ♥ ♥ ♥ ♥
Taurus	♥ ♡ ♡ ♡ ♡	Scorpio	♥ ♥ ♡ ♡ ♡
Gemini	♥ ♥ ♥ ♥ ♥	Sagittarius	♥ ♥ ♥ ♥ ♡
Cancer	♥ ♥ ♡ ♡ ♡	Capricorn	♥ ♥ ♡ ♡ ♡
Leo	♥ ♥ ♥ ♥ ♡	Aquarius	♥ ♥ ♥ ♡ ♡
Virgo	♥ ♥ ♡ ♡ ♡	Pisces	♥ ♥ ♡ ♡ ♡

MANTRA I am   **POWER** Action

KEYWAORD Assert   **ANATOMY** Head, Face, Brain

LIGHT
Pioneer
Competitive
Executive
Impulsive
Courageous
Independent
Dynamic
Lives in the present
Fast

SHADOW
Domineering
Irascible
Violent
Intolerant
Rushed
Arrogant
"Me first"
Rude
Has no persistence

Meditation for the month of Nissan
Scan with your eyes from right to left

A R I E S

MARCH 21ST – 5:23PM (UTC) – 0° ARIES

Los Angeles (UTC -7) • New York (UTC -4) • London (UTC +0)
Paris (UTC +1) • Sydney (UTC +10)

SET YOUR INTENTIONS FOR THE NEXT 6 MONTHS

HOW ARE YOU GOING TO GET THERE?

Open paths	New adventures	Willpower
Entrepreneurship	Physical energy	Dynamic
In charge	Risk-taker	Unstoppable
Competitive	Optimism	Pushy

MAR
19
SUN

☿ ♈
Mercury enters Aries until 3rd April

After all the distraction of last week, now
our mind becomes more agile and our plans
seem to want to jump out of our brain. Get
organized to direct your impulses toward
something that is worth the investment.

☽ ♓
Moon in Pisces

⊙ ♓ ✳ ♇ ♑
Sun in Pisces sextile Pluto in Capricorn

MAR
20
MON

Monday starts with total focus because we have a
dream that we want to manifest this year. Time to
investigate what the biggest plan is that you want to
see come true in your life. Write down your biggest
dreams here, and who can help you with them.

⊙ ♈
Sun enters Aries
Spring Equinox – North Hemisphere
Ostara Festival

Happy astrological New Year! The Sun has turned
full circle in the Zodiac and today we start a new
cycle. We enter a new season, saying goodbye to
the old and to what no longer serves us. Make a
beautiful ritual to welcome the next seaso

Moon   s

S S M T W T F S S M T W T F S S M T W T F S S M   T F S S M
1 2 3 4 5 6 7 8 9 10 11 12 13 14 15 16 17 18 19 20 21 22 23 2   27 28 29 30 31

MAR
21
TUE

New Moon 0º Aries

The Sun enters and soon the Moon follows,
together in the 0th degree of Aries. It's as if
we reset all the stories of the past and are
ready, dressed in white, for the new! Plant
the seeds of this new cycle using the New
Moon page. Everything that is born now has
the boost to become a great enterprise.

MAR
22
WED

☽ ♈
Moon in Aries

MAR
23
THU

♇ ♒
Pluto enters Aquarius until 11th June (will retrograde)

On 27 November 2008 Pluto landed in Capricorn and stayed there for 15 years! Now it's time to peek into what awaits us in this next cycle. We have three months to discover our long-awaited freedom, innovate as a collective and create new laws that embrace all our diversity.

☽ ♉
Moon in Taurus

MAR
24
FRI

☽ ♉
Moon in Taurus

MAR
25
SAT

♂ ♋
Mars enters Cancer until 20th May

Saturday is a little dramatic as our
action and direction becomes a bit more
temperamental. Good for research and
elaborate studies, taking care of our
property and land, but avoid unnecessary
family dramas. We are more needy and
looking to the past more than usual.

☽ ♊
Moon in Gemini

MAR
26
SUN

☽ ♊
Moon in Gemini

MAR

27

MON

☽ ♊
Moon in Gemini

MAR

28

TUE

☿ ☌ ♃ ♈
Mercury meets Jupiter in Aries

Good Tuesday for all intellectual work,
writing, thinking and publishing. Our mind is
faster than ever and Jupiter helps us to have
the good luck needed to be in the right place
at the right time. Beware of accidents, and
take care that all the ideas going through your
mind now don't bring on a physical headache!

☽ ♋
Moon in Cancer

MAR
29
WED

◐ ♋
First Quarter 8º Cancer

Once again the past is calling us to
attention. Some old love crashes back
into your heart. Some addictive affection
is still insisting and making it grow.
Allow only what values you to blossom.

MAR
30
THU

♂ ♋ △ ♄ ♓
Mars in Cancer trine Saturn in Pisces

Something you've been working on or
researching for a while receives a boost of
divine help! It's the stars telling you to believe
in your dreams, something you value a lot is
ready to be appreciated by the world! Enjoy!

♀ ♂ ♅ ♉
Venus meets Uranus in Taurus

Day to sell online, good for all activities
that include beauty, arts, finance. The
financial market can be pretty crazy
today – don't invest without caution.

☽ ♌
Moon in Leo

MAR
31
FRI

☽ ♌
Moon in Leo

MON	TUE	WED

AP RIL

the first day
of the month
starts with the
ephemeris

⊙ 11º ♈

☽ 18º ♌

☿ 26º ♈

♀ 18º ♉

♂ 3º ♋

♃ 19º ♈

♄ 2º ♓

♅ 16º ♉

♆ 25º ♓

♇ 0º ♒

MON	TUE	WED
03	04	05
10	11	12
17	18	19
24	25	26

THU	FRI	SAT	SUN
		01	02
06	07	08	09
13	14	15	16
20	21	22	23
27	28	29	30

APR

01
SAT

☽ ♌
Moon in Leo

APR

02
SUN

☽ ♍
Moon in Virgo

S S M T W T F S S M T W T F S S M T W T F S S M T W T F S S
1 2 3 4 5 6 7 8 9 10 11 12 13 14 15 16 17 18 19 20 21 22 23 24 25 26 27 28 29 30

APR
03
MON

☿ ♉
Mercury enters Taurus until 11th June (will retrograde)

Mercury wants to root its ideals and thoughts now. We
become more stable and are given a break from the
anxiety of the last days. Our memory is much better now,
and we are capable of any sustained mental work.

☿ ♉ □ ♇ ♒
Mercury in Taurus squares Pluto in Aquarius

Right on his arrival in Taurus, Mercury meets Pluto to think
together about the new laws that will govern this new world
panorama and the new society. On a personal level it could mean
new natural laws that we will prefer to follow from now on.

☽ ♍
Moon in Virgo

APR
04
TUE

☽ ♎
Moon in Libra

APR
05
WED

☿ ♉ ✳ ♄ ♓
Mercury in Taurus sextile Saturn in Pisces

Excellent aspect to bring to Earth what
before was only an illusion or fantasy.
Saturn is close to dreams but Mercury
wants to act in practical ways. Think
of ways to further realize and manifest
the reality you so desperately desire.

☽ ♎
Moon in Libra

APR
06
THU

○ ♎
Full Moon 16º Libra

This is a great Full Moon to examine the dynamics
within our closest relationships and communicate
openly about our interpersonal issues. As the
cardinal air sign of the zodiac, Libra's energy inspires
us to smooth over any disagreements.

APR

07

FRI

♀ ♉ ✳ Ψ ♓
Venus in Taurus sextile Neptune in Pisces

Super passionate and romantic Friday. Call your
love to go out and enjoy an evening under the Stars
together. Poetry, music, bring flowers and scented
candles to toast this beautiful moment in the sky.

☽ ♏
Moon in Scorpio

APR

08

SAT

☿ ♉ ✳ ♂ ♋
Mercury in Taurus sextile Mars in Cancer

An old project that is very important to you
begins to take root and you want to put your
structures down even deeper. A good Saturday
to bring even more substance to an old idea.

☽ ♏
Moon in Scorpio

S S M T W T F S S M T W T F S S M T W T F S S M T W T F S S
1 2 3 4 5 6 7 8 9 10 11 12 13 14 15 16 17 18 19 20 21 22 23 24 25 26 27 28 29 30

APR

09
SUN

☽ ♐
Moon in Sagittarius

APR

10
MON

☽ ♐
Moon in Sagittarius

S S M T W T F S S M T W T F S S M T W T F S S M T W T F S S
1 2 3 4 5 6 7 8 9 10 11 12 13 14 15 16 17 18 19 20 21 22 23 24 25 26 27 28 29 30

♀ ♊
Venus enters Gemini until 7th May

APR
11
TUE

Venus in Gemini becomes even more
curious and mystical. Time to learn
more about some esoteric subjects.

♀ ♊ △ ♇ ♒
Venus in Gemini trine Pluto in Aquarius

Something that was once a hobby could become
your official source of income. Don't underestimate
your will to learn about a variety of subjects.

☉ ♂ ♃ ♈
Sun meets Jupiter in Aries

Sun and Jupiter will reinforce
the need to learn and share.

☽ ♑
Moon in Capricorn

APR
12
WED

☽ ♑
Moon in Capricorn

APR

13

THU

◑ ♑
Last Quarter 23º Capricorn

Old structures that are saying goodbye open up physical space for new constructions, new furniture, new material acquisitions. Just be careful with expenses.

APR

14

FRI

♀ ♊ □ ♄ ♓
Venus in Gemini squares Saturn in Pisces

Saturn allows Venus to have fun but warns you not to waste your energy and not to devalue yourself with those who do not have the same vibration. Be close to the ones who deserve you and believe in you.

☽ ♒
Moon in Aquarius

APR

15

SAT

☽ ♓
Moon in Pisces

APR

16

SUN

☽ ♓
Moon in Pisces

APR

17

MON

☽ ♈
Moon in Aries

APR

18

TUE

☽ ♈
Moon in Aries

Meditation for the month of Iyyar
Scan with your eyes from right to left

A R I E S

APRIL 20TH – 4:12AM (UTC) – 29° ARIES ECLIPSE ANNULAR TOTAL
Los Angeles (UTC -7) • New York (UTC -4) • London (UTC +1) • Paris (UTC +2) • Sydney (UTC +10)

SET YOUR INTENTIONS FOR THE NEXT 6 MONTHS

_____

_____

_____

_____

_____

HOW ARE YOU GOING TO GET THERE?

_____

_____

_____

_____

_____

New cycle	Passion	Accept risks
Energy of beginnings	New image	Challenge yourself
Impulse	Initiative and proactivity	New developments
Strength and courage	Leadership	Physical training

TAURUS

April 20th / 08:14am (UTC)

EARTH

VENUS

TAURUS

MODE Fixed	**ELEMENT** Earth	**RULING PLANET** Venus

CRYSTAL Emerald   **BACH FLOWER REMEDY** Gentian

PRINCIPLE Negative   **OPPOSITE SIGN** Scorpio

TAURUS AND SIGNS IN LOVE

Aries	♥ ♡ ♡ ♡ ♡	Libra	♥ ♥ ♥ ♥ ♡
Taurus	♥ ♥ ♥ ♥ ♡	Scorpio	♥ ♥ ♥ ♥ ♥
Gemini	♥ ♥ ♡ ♡ ♡	Sagittarius	♥ ♡ ♡ ♡ ♡
Cancer	♥ ♥ ♥ ♡ ♡	Capricorn	♥ ♥ ♥ ♡ ♡
Leo	♥ ♥ ♥ ♥ ♡	Aquarius	♥ ♥ ♡ ♡ ♡
Virgo	♥ ♥ ♥ ♥ ♥	Pisces	♥ ♥ ♥ ♥ ♡

MANTRA I have   **POWER** Stability

KEYWORD Possess   **ANATOMY** Neck, Ears, Vocal cords, Thyroid, Tongue, Throat, Mouth, Tonsils

LIGHT
Patient
Conservative
Sensual
Scrupulous
Stable
Trustworthy
Practical
Loyal

SHADOW
Self-indulgent
Stubborn
Slow
Prone to gossip
Irascible
Possessive
Glutton
Materialist

APR
19
WED

● ♈
New Moon Annular Total Eclipse 29º Aries

Second New Moon in Aries, this time Total Eclipse! A part
of us has to leave the scene now: a long-pursued ideal,
something that it no longer makes sense to carry forward. We
strip off those old costumes to walk toward our destiny.

APR
20
THU

☉ ♉
Sun enters Taurus

Right after yesterday's intense Eclipse, we need to
recharge our strength, maybe closer to nature. The Sun in
Taurus calls for healthy eating, a deeper connection with
Mother Earth and for us to look at our own inner treasures.

☉ ♉ □ ♇ ♒
Sun in Taurus squares Pluto in Aquarius

Pluto also questions us about our values, how we
negotiate our individuality with the collective. A great
time to make your contribution to a better society.

☽ ♉
Moon in Taurus

APR
21
FRI

☿ St ℞ ♉
Mercury Stations Retrograde (Rx) in 15º Taurus

After so much nervousness, Mercury prepares for
a pause. We put our foot on the brake of the plans;
we will restructure the planning for the next 23 days.

☽ ♉
Moon in Taurus

APR
22
SAT

☿ ℞ ♉
Mercury Rx in Taurus until 15th May

Still on the theme of self-worth, now is the
time to rethink our confidence, the confidence
we have in what we say and think. Do you
really act exactly as you think or how you tell
other people to act? Think about it.

☽ ♊
Moon in Gemini

APR
23
SUN

☽ ♊
Moon in Gemini

APR
24
MON

☿ ℞ ♉ ✳ ♂ ♋
Mercury Rx in Taurus sextile Mars in
Cancer (2nd time – 8th April)

Another conversation with Mars about
that old project which is very important
to you. Time to reprogramme the
strategy, to become even more solid.

☽ ♋
Moon in Cancer

S S M T W T F S S M T W T F S S M T W T F S S M T W T F S S
1 2 3 4 5 6 7 8 9 10 11 12 13 14 15 16 17 18 19 20 21 22 23 24 25 26 27 28 29 30

APR
25
TUE

☉ ♉ ✱ ♄ ♓
Sun in Taurus sextile Saturn in Pisces

Without self-esteem we can't make the necessary inversion to transform an ideal into something real. You need to work on your inner security before showing yourself to the world. Say in front of the mirror: I deserve the life I dream of.

☽ ♋
Moon in Cancer

APR
26
WED

☽ ♋
Moon in Cancer

APR
27
THU

◗ ♌
First Quarter 7º Leo

Remember how easy it was in childhood to
imagine how the future would be, without
worries, just enjoying moments of achievements.
Do a meditation, with childlike eyes, for what
you wish to manifest this year in your life. Play,
dance and get your pure heart beating again.

APR
28
FRI

☽ ♌
Moon in Leo

APR
29
SAT

♂ ♋ ✳ ♅ ♉
Mars in Cancer sextile Uranus in Taurus

In the midst of the construction of our
plans, there are always surprises that may
or may not be pleasant. Don't be upset if
someone doesn't value your idea. When
one door closes, two others may open.

☽ ♍
Moon in Virgo

APR
30
SUN

☽ ♍
Moon in Virgo

MAY

the first day
of the month
starts with the
ephemeris

☉ 10º ♉

☽ 20º ♍

☿ᴿ 12º ♉

♀ 23º ♊

♂ 19º ♋

♃ 26º ♈

♄ 5º ♓

♅ 18º ♉

♆ 26º ♓

♇ 0º ♒

MON	TUE	WED
01	02	03
08	09	10
15	16	17
22	23	24
29	30	31

THU	FRI	SAT	SUN
04	05	06	07
11	12	13	14
18	19	20	21
25	26	27	28

MAY
01
MON

♇ St ℞ ♒
Pluto Stations Retrograde 0° Aquarius

We have reached that part of the year
when we descend the ladder toward
our depths. Time to face our shadows!

☉ ☌ ☿ ℞ ♉
Sun meets Mercury Rx in Taurus

Sun and Mercury Rx meet to mark the
halfway point of the retrograde. From
now on we already have more concrete
ideas on how to express ourselves with
more authority – we can already feel
safe in our thoughts and speech.

☽ ♍
Moon in Virgo

MAY
02
TUE

♇ ℞ ♒
Pluto Retrograde in Aquarius until 11th October

We have five months to find our inner
treasures, rediscover our strength,
organize the structure that supports us
and come back even more powerful after
this season. Seek help: therapy and a talk
with a specialist can work miracles!

☽ ♎
Moon in Libra

MAY

03

WED

☽ ♎︎
Moon in Libra

MAY

04

THU

♀ ♊︎ □ ♆ ♓︎
Venus in Gemini squares Neptune in Pisces

Perfect day for creation, arts, music. Our energy
is unfocused but very creative. Not a good time for
more serious presentations that require a lot of
attention to detail. Don't book meetings on this day.

☽ ♏︎
Moon in Scorpio

MAY
05
FRI

♀ ♊ ✳ ♃ ♈
Venus in Gemini sextile Jupiter in Aries

Full Moon Friday and Venus is bustling around, wanting to socialize with as many people as possible. There may be a question about which partner is right for you at this time, or perhaps there are so many options it's hard to choose. Which partner values you the most? Don't create an atmosphere of jealousy as the evening promises to be magickal and sensual.

○ ♏
Full Moon 14º Scorpio

Vesak Day! Full Moon of blessings of Buddha, as we celebrate his enlightenment, death and rebirth. Time to rebirth our hopes for more enlightened days, looking at our shadows and welcoming our fear of ending cycles. Excellent for blessing all relationships, celebrate the magick of being together living this moment on Earth.

MAY
06
SAT

☽ ♐
Moon in Sagittarius

MAY

07

SUN

♀ ♋
Venus enters Cancer until 5th June

After a super intense Full Moon, and a very exposed and social season, Venus enters Cancer and just wants a nice cosy snug place, comfort food, cuddling and a love nest. Create that space to enjoy the next few days, even if it's in your own company.

☽ ♐
Moon in Sagittarius

MAY

08

MON

☽ ♑
Moon in Capricorn

MAY
09
TUE

☉ ♂ ♅ ♉
Sun meets Uranus in Taurus

Nervous and electric Tuesday, excellent
for all technological endeavours, electronic
presentations; anything involving Uranian
cleverness gains power. There could be
some impact on digital currencies, or the
tech market. Expect surprises!

☽ ♑
Moon in Capricorn

MAY
10
WED

☽ ♒
Moon in Aquarius

MAY

11

THU

☽ ≈
Moon in Aquarius

☿ R ♉ ⚹ ♄ ♓
Mercury Rx in Taurus sextile Saturn in Pisces
(2nd – 5th April)

MAY

12

FRI

Last chance to revise documents, review your plans and
commit yourself again, now more clearly, to everything
that depends on you from now on! Prepare everything,
but wait until next week to take action and have the
conversations that need your attention now. Good luck!

☿ R ♉ ⚹ ♀ ♋
Mercury Rx in Taurus sextile Venus in Cancer

Take the opportunity to redo your wish list: the things
you wanted to manifest in your life at the beginning of
the year may no longer enchant you! You have a much
clearer idea of the kind of conversation you need to have in
relationships, but again, wait until Monday to take a stand.

◑ ≈
Last Quarter 21º Aquarius

The Moon losing light in Aquarius. Excellent time to leave a
habit behind, something you used to do almost instinctively
no longer makes sense. Leave it behind and move on!

MAY

13

SAT

♀ ♋ △ ♄ ♓
Venus in Cancer trine Saturn in Pisces

Saturday is the day to commit to an old dream
of the heart. It could be that a relationship is
taking a more real form now, or that you are
dreaming big about an ideal of love. Saturn
helps you to make this dream come true.

☽ ♓
Moon in Pisces

MAY

14

SUN

☿ St D ♉
Mercury St Direct in 5º Taurus

Mercury is getting ready to wake up
and put down deeper roots in our
ideals of life and security. Today the
energy is still intense – prepare this
week to be firm in your next decisions!

☽ ♓
Moon in Pisces

♂ ♋ △ Ψ ♓
Mars in Cancer trine Neptune in Pisces

An old project involving your spirituality or alternative therapies, your self-knowledge wants to be born through you. Stop for a moment today to close your eyes and receive divine insights. The Cosmos and your guardian angels have an important message to send you and they cannot wait any longer.

☿ D ♉
Mercury Direct in Taurus

From now on it will be much easier to communicate and be objective when the subject is finance or even the beginning of something great that you wish to manifest. Green light to sign everything that was waiting for your decision. Invest in your equipment: now is the time to renew your work instruments.

☽ ♈
Moon in Aries

♃ ♉
Jupiter enters Taurus until 25th May 2024

Jupiter, the giant of the heavens, arrives in the fertile territory of Taurus to grow the seeds of a new economy, a greater care for the environment and our lands. All fields dealing with agriculture, growing food, the natural, organic, handmade and finances will be blessed, as a new economy should be born in the coming months. We will be watching!

☽ ♈
Moon in Aries

M T W T F S S M T W T F S S M T W T F S S M T W T F S S M T W
1 2 3 4 5 **6 7** 8 9 10 11 12 **13 14** 15 16 17 18 19 **20 21** 22 23 24 25 26 **27 28** 29 30 31

MAY
17
WED

♃ ♉ □ ♇ ℞ ♒
Jupiter in Taurus squares Pluto Rx in Aquarius

Jupiter in Taurus wants to propose an agrarian reform, a better distribution of resources, land and finances, and Pluto, newly arrived in Aquarius, also wants to be revolutionary, but an agreement between the two seems difficult. Each one wants to enforce their own law, and the stubbornness ends up winning. Put your weapons aside – you don't want to exploit others for your own benefit.

☽ ♉
Moon in Taurus

MAY
18
THU

☉ ♉ ✳ ♆ ♓
Sun in Taurus sextile Neptune in Pisces

A special day to help you manifest your high ideals. Good for writers and artists, an important aspect to blow off steam and find a common denominator. Today it's easier to negotiate your value and dreams!

☽ ♉
Moon in Taurus

Meditation for the month of Sivan
Scan with your eyes from right to left

T A U R U S

MAY 19TH – 3:53PM (UTC) – 28° TAURUS
Los Angeles (UTC -7) • New York (UTC -4) • London (UTC +1)
Paris (UTC +2) • Sydney (UTC +10)

SET YOUR INTENTIONS FOR THE NEXT 6 MONTHS

HOW ARE YOU GOING TO GET THERE?

Safety	Stability	Sensuality
Productivity	Financial resources	Self esteem
Persistence	Intimacy	Body aesthetics
Values	Pleasure	Comfort

MAY
19
FRI

☿ ♉ ✳ ♄ ♓
Mercury in Taurus sextile Saturn in Pisces
(3rd – 5th April / 12th May)

On this third date we are more practical and logical and
have easy access to speech that comes from the heart.
Our mind is more disciplined and willing to touch deep
into the soul of the listeners, with responsibility and
wisdom. Good for touching speeches and presentations.

● ♉
New Moon 28º Taurus

Plant the seeds for your material security to be
even more prevalent. Defend your values and don't
let anyone underestimate you. Treat your senses
with a good meal in a comfortable and pleasing
environment. Listen to great music. Today we
intend a safer and more pleasant world for all.

♂ ♌
Mars enters Leo until 20th May

MAY
20
SAT

Mars in Leo is ardent! Fun-loving, party-going,
dynamic, you now pick up some of this vibe and
exhale magnetism wherever you go. A strong
attraction pushes you to seek partnerships as warm
as your generous heart desires. Self-confidence is
running high – try to think about developing more
humility at each step of this process.

♂ ♌ ☍ ♇ ℞ ♒
Mars in Leo opposite Pluto Rx in Aquarius

And at the entrance of the sign of Leo, Mars, who
is already overconfident, finds a worthy opponent.
It's an aspect that asks us to be careful how we
treat people; we might be more arrogant than usual.
Channel this powerful energy in an intense night of
love with your partner, but avoid misunderstandings.

☽ ♊
Moon in Gemini

MAY

21

SUN

☉ ♊
Sun enters Gemini

We welcome the most buzzing and social month
of the year! The agility with which time is passing
brings us a bit of a rush as we have so many people
to contact, meet, exchange with. Variety is the tone
of this month. You may feel a little unfocused but
you're certainly more expressive than usual. Take the
opportunity to activate your network of contacts!

☉ ♊ △ ♇ ℞ ♒
Sun in Gemini trine Pluto Rx in Aquarius

Make a list of the most important people you have in
your circle of friends, or the groups of important people
you'd like to join. Start a conversation with these people,
send them an email, schedule an event to strengthen
ties. Be surrounded by those who want your success,
focus on friendships that are worth keeping.

☽ ♊
Moon in Gemini

MAY

22

MON

☉ ♊ ✶ ♂ ♌
Sun in Gemini sextile Mars in Leo

How about promoting a meeting between your friends and
creating a real network of important people? Introduce friends
to each other, make an event for everyone to get to know each
other, asking them to bring interesting people to the event as well.
Today is a great day to exchange information and spread your
knowledge throughout your crew. The Full Moon in Sagittarius
next Saturday is a good time for this exchange of contacts.

☽ ♋
Moon in Cancer

GEMINI

May 21st / 07:09am (UTC)

AIR

MERCURY

GEMINI

MODE Mutable	**ELEMENT** Air	**RULING PLANET** Mercury

CRYSTAL Agate   **BACH FLOWER REMEDY** Cerato

PRINCIPLE Positive   **OPPOSITE SIGN** Sagittarius

GEMINI AND SIGNS IN LOVE

Aries	♥ ♥ ♥ ♥ ♡	Libra	♥ ♥ ♥ ♥ ♥
Taurus	♥ ♥ ♡ ♡ ♡	Scorpio	♥ ♡ ♡ ♡ ♡
Gemini	♥ ♥ ♥ ♥ ♥	Sagittarius	♥ ♥ ♥ ♥ ♥
Cancer	♥ ♡ ♡ ♡ ♡	Capricorn	♥ ♡ ♡ ♡ ♡
Leo	♥ ♥ ♥ ♡ ♡	Aquarius	♥ ♥ ♥ ♥ ♡
Virgo	♥ ♥ ♥ ♡ ♡	Pisces	♥ ♥ ♡ ♡ ♡

MANTRA I think   **POWER** Versatility

KEYWORD Communicate **ANATOMY** Lungs, Arms, Shoulders, Nervous System

LIGHT	**SHADOW**
Social	Changeable
Curious	Ungrateful
Adaptable	Senseless
Expressive	Restless
Inventive	Conniving
Intelligent	No concentration

MAY

23

TUE

♂ ♌ □ ♃ ♉
Mars in Leo squares Jupiter in Taurus

To succeed with your plans, you need to inject a little
more discipline or they will get out of hand. Don't
waste your ideas impulsively – plan for enjoyment and
the multiplication of your sources of funds will follow.
Beware of exaggerations, especially financial ones.

☽ ♋
Moon in Cancer

MAY

24

WED

☽ ♌
Moon in Leo

MAY
25
THU

☽ ♌
Moon in Leo

MAY
26
FRI

♀ ♋ ✳ ⛢ ♉
Venus in Cancer sextile Uranus in Taurus

A flash romance could strike right at the core
of your heart. Or someone from the past
knocks on your door again and surprises you
with a declaration of love. Analyse carefully
what this person means to you and what they
can add to your life from now on.

☽ ♌
Moon in Leo

MAY

27

SAT

◑ ♍
First Quarter 6º Virgo

Cultivate the seeds that you planted with the intention of helping others, but give up a little bit of control and don't require things to be done the way you want, at the time you want. Replace restlessness with steadiness and practicality. Great day for a Tarot reading, aura reading or any esoteric activity.

MAY

28

SUN

☉ ♊ □ ♄ ♓
Sun in Gemini squares Saturn in Pisces

Sunday, where our expression is a little limited, we may want to be alone or feel a little unsupported. A mean comment can make you a bit more timid, but don't fall into the traps of your mind. Tomorrow the Sun rises again!

☽ ♍
Moon in Virgo

MAY
29
MON

☽ ♎
Moon in Libra

MAY
30
TUE

☽ ♎
Moon in Libra

☽ ♏
Moon in Scorpio

MON	TUE	WED
JUNE		

the first day
of the month
starts with the
ephemeris

☉ 10º ♊

☽ 6º ♏

☿ 16º ♉

♀ 26º ♋

♂ 6º ♌

♃ 3º ♉

♄ 7º ♓

♅ 20º ♉

♆ 27º ♓

♇ᴿ 0º ♒

MON	TUE	WED
05	06	07
12	13	14
19	20	21
26	27	28

THU	FRI	SAT	SUN
01	02	03	04
08	09	10	11
15	16	17	18
22	23	24	25
29	30		

JUN
01
THU

☽ ♏
Moon in Scorpio

JUN
02
FRI

♀ ♋ △ ♆ ♓
Venus in Cancer trine Neptune in Pisces

Venus transiting Cancer could surprise you
with pleasant weekends in the company
of those you love most. This is another
romantic Friday full of love and comfort.
Be in a cosy environment and talk about
your dreams to someone. Write about love!

☽ ♏
Moon in Scorpio

T F S S M T W T F S S M T W T F S S M T W T F S S M T W T F
1 2 3 4 5 6 7 8 9 10 11 12 13 14 15 16 17 18 19 20 21 22 23 24 25 26 27 28 29 30

JUN

03

SAT

Full Moon 13º Sagittarius

Today is a day of celebration in the sky! With the Full Moon
connecting people, goals, different paths, tonight promises to be
democratic. Excellent to be among various cultures, discussing
deep issues, exchanging life impressions. You may be celebrating
an achievement far from home, perhaps in another country.
Celebrate and have fun, and try not to get too over-excited.

JUN

04

SUN

☿ ♂ ♅ ♉

Mercury meets Uranus in Taurus

Mercury could bring you breaking news or
perhaps a big negotiation suddenly appears. If
you didn't overdo it yesterday, this could be a
very welcome surprise, so be prepared.

☽ ♐

Moon in Sagittarius

JUN
05
MON

♀ ♌
Venus enters Leo until 8th October (will retrograde)

In her last retrogradation in 2021, Venus was seeking stability
in career and finances, creating a new structure in our lives.
Now she wants to review her talents and rediscover what
makes our hearts beat faster. Time to look at your inner child
and remember what your childhood wishes were, those
which can come true in your present life.

♀ ♌ ☍ ♇ ℞ ♒
Venus in Leo opposite Pluto Rx in Aquarius

The planets change signs and end up meeting Pluto for a very
frank conversation. Venus looks at her talents but Pluto wants
her to share them with the world and not just her small circle
of friends. Time to think about how to present your greatest
treasures on a global level, for a whole society to appreciate.

☽ ♑
Moon in Capricorn

JUN
06
TUE

☽ ♑
Moon in Capricorn

JUN
07
WED

☽ ≋
Moon in Aquarius

JUN
08
THU

☽ ≋
Moon in Aquarius

JUN
09
FRI

☿ ♉ ✷ ♆ ♓
Mercury in Taurus sextile Neptune in Pisces

A good Friday for negotiating our values and making great transactions. Our imagination is super focused and we can be more convinced of our competence to get there. Great day for sales, deals, bazaars, shops and every monetary exchange you want to make.

☽ ♓
Moon in Pisces

✦

JUN
10
SAT

◑ ♓
Last Quarter 19º Pisces

A slightly melancholic Saturday: we are very sensitive and our emotional wounds may want to emerge again. Let go of everything that no longer serves you, let go, cry, listen to a sad song to help you put it aside. Allow yourself to be free!

♇ ℞ ♑
Pluto Rx goes back to Capricorn until 20th January 2024

JUN
11
SUN

We have had two and a half months to taste a little of this revolution that Pluto wants to organize in Aquarius, starting next year. We can expect great planetary changes and changes in society, in laws and in the constitution. The world is shifting and we need to vibrate – may it be for the better!

☿ ♉ △ ♇ ℞ ♑
Mercury in Taurus trine Pluto Rx in Capricorn

One minute before entering Gemini, stubborn Mercury wants to confirm with Pluto its old intentions. There are some old ideals that are worth taking into the New Age.

☿ ♊
Mercury enters Gemini until 26th June

Mercury enters one of its houses and we gain mental agility and a great ability to express ourselves. We are more inclined to take short trips, study and reading are highly recommended. The interests are such that we develop two or more skills at the same time, change our minds quickly and become multi-taskers in the blink of an eye!

♀ ♌ □ ♃ ♉
Venus in Leo squares Jupiter in Taurus

Beware of extravagance, of overspending. You don't want to appear to have more than you really have. It makes us want to attract attention for the most trivial reasons. Don't fall into this ego trap.

☽ ♈
Moon in Aries

JUN
12
MON

☽ ♈
Moon in Aries

JUN
13
TUE

☽ ♉
Moon in Taurus

JUN
14
WED

☽ ♉
Moon in Taurus

JUN
15
THU

☿ ♊ □ ♄ ♓
Mercury in Gemini squares Saturn in Pisces

Our mind is too fast and our desires are too many.
The commitments we take on may be more than we
can handle, and this creates great anxiety. Just take a
deep breath, make a list of priorities and complete one
step at a time. Don't commit to anything else for now:
finish the work you started and calm your mind.

☽ ♊
Moon in Gemini

JUN
16
FRI

☽ ♊
Moon in Gemini

JUN
17
SAT

☿ ♊ ⚹ ♀ ♌
Mercury in Gemini sextile Venus in Leo

Magnificent day for presentations, oratory, performances, theatre,
cinema, music. We are sociable and quite expressive, everything
is in order for those who wish to impact others with their talents.

♄ St ℞ ♓
Saturn Stations Retrograde 7º Pisces

Saturn prepares to review the many thousands of
commitments you have made since the beginning
of the year. Time to give pause to new agreements.

♄ ℞ ♓
Saturn Retrograde in Pisces until 4th November

JUN
18
SUN

From now until November, we do not make any more big serious
commitments, like buying a house, a financial or business agreement or a
marriage. We use these five months to review our degree of commitment to
everything that we have already taken responsibility for to this moment.

⊙ ♊ □ ♆ ♓
Sun in Gemini squares Neptune in Pisces

Your intentions are noble, but a lack of confidence may be sabotaging your
long-term plans. Don't underestimate your capacity for success. You may
be carrying too much weight, but take it easy – we are more emotional than
usual today.

● ♊
New Moon 26º Gemini

With the New Moon in Gemini, every artistic project that starts today has the
power to spread very quickly and gain the fame that Venus in Leo desires
so much.

☽ ♋
Moon in Cancer

זאת

יהוה

Meditation for the month of Tamuz
Scan with your eyes from right to left

G E M I N I

JUNE 18TH – 4:37AM (UTC) – 26° GEMINI

Los Angeles (UTC -7) • New York (UTC -4) • London (UTC +1)
Paris (UTC +2) • Sydney (UTC +10)

SET YOUR INTENTIONS FOR THE NEXT 6 MONTHS

HOW ARE YOU GOING TO GET THERE?

Flexibility	Social work	Connect people
Adaptability	Curiosity	Learning
Cunning	Communication	Express yourself
Persuasion	Quickness	Youth

JUN
19
MON

Jupiter in Taurus sextile Saturn Rx in Pisces

We've started the week very well and are looking
very lucky! Perhaps a past commitment is starting
to pay off and you can already feel life flowing with
more abundance. Take time to meditate on your
aspirations and your quest for material security.

☽ ♋
Moon in Cancer

JUN
20
TUE

☽ ♌
Moon in Leo

JUN
21
WED

☿ ♊ ＊ ♂ ♌
Mercury in Gemini sextile Mars in Leo

Our mind is more powerful than anything. We don't ever want to stop learning but to stand out on our merits. This is a day to receive an award, to shine with an innovative idea, to gain visibility for something that came from your heart. Have the courage to be who you are!

☉ ♋
Sun enters Cancer
Summer Solstice – North Hemisphere
Litha Festival

The Sun touches the sign of Cancer and a nostalgia can accompany us. It is the beginning of a new season, where we can be closer to those we love. Leave shyness aside and don't worry about what others think of you. Bring your friends for a cosy dinner at home, or seek a quiet refuge to enjoy these first days of a new time!

☽ ♌
Moon in Leo

JUN
22
THU

☽ ♌
Moon in Leo

CANCER

June 21st / 2:58pm (UTC)

WATER

MOON

CANCER

MODE Cardinal	**ELEMENT** Water	**RULING PLANET** Moon

CRYSTAL Moon Stone   **BACH FLOWER REMEDY** Clematis

PRINCIPLE Negative   **OPPOSITE SIGN** Capricorn

CANCER AND SIGNS IN LOVE

Sign	Hearts	Sign	Hearts
Aries	♥ ♡ ♡ ♡ ♡	Libra	♥ ♥ ♥ ♡ ♡
Taurus	♥ ♥ ♥ ♥ ♡	Scorpio	♥ ♥ ♥ ♥ ♥
Gemini	♥ ♡ ♡ ♡ ♡	Sagittarius	♥ ♡ ♡ ♡ ♡
Cancer	♥ ♥ ♥ ♥ ♡	Capricorn	♥ ♥ ♥ ♥ ♡
Leo	♥ ♥ ♥ ♡ ♡	Aquarius	♥ ♥ ♡ ♡ ♡
Virgo	♥ ♥ ♥ ♥ ♡	Pisces	♥ ♥ ♥ ♥ ♥

MANTRA I feel   **POWER** Devotion

KEYWORD Feeling   **ANATOMY** Stomach, Pancreas, Chest

LIGHT	SHADOW
Tenacious	Touchy
Maternal	Hurts easily
Sensitive	Negative
Retentive	Manipulative
Helps others	Too cautious
Friendly	Lazy
Emotional	Selfish
Patriotic	Self-pitying
Traditional	Insecure
Good memory	Passive

JUN
23
FRI

☽ ♍
Moon in Virgo

JUN
24
SAT

☽ ♍
Moon in Virgo

JUN
25
SUN

☿ Ⅱ □ Ψ ♓
Mercury in Gemini squares Neptune in Pisces

Distraction and dissipation today – good thing
it's a Sunday and we can rest and meditate.
Painting, dancing, social programmes and
music are all welcome, but beware of
deception; you may be too distracted today!

☽ ♎
Moon in Libra

JUN
26
MON

♂ ♌ □ ♅ ♉
Mars in Leo squares Uranus in Taurus

An important aspect that can help you become a leader.
However, it can also make us even more impulsive, so
learn to control yourself and victory will be assured.

☿ ♋
Mercury enters Cancer until 11th July

After a tense moment in the sky, we may want to
look for answers in our past attitudes. A good time to
remember old stories and evaluate our behaviour today
compared with previous actions. Feeling the rhythm of
the Universe is essential to overcome challenges.

◐ ♎
First Quarter 4º Libra

Intend better relationships. Grow your will to share
even more of your intimacy with someone special,
or to associate with the best partner in business.
All relationships gain a drive to be even better.

JUN
27
TUE

☽ ♎
Moon in Libra

JUN
28
WED

☉ ♋ △ ♄ ℞ ♓
Sun in Cancer trine Saturn Rx in Pisces

Good aspect to commit even more to old dreams
and plans. Their success and realization depends
on your effort alone, and your ability to research,
analyse and plan the next steps. Trust the Universe!

☽ ♏
Moon in Scorpio

JUN
29
THU

☽ ♏︎
Moon in Scorpio

JUN
30
FRI

☿ ♋︎ △ ♄ ℞ ♓︎
Mercury in Cancer trine Saturn Rx in Pisces

Capacity for maximum concentration, excellent for
artistic studies or learning a new hobby. Great gains
for all work involving research, archives, memory,
antiquity, family roots. Enjoy the concentration and
dive deeper into your research.

♆ St ℞ ♓︎
Neptune Stations Retrograde 27º Pisces

Neptune prepares for its six-month deep
dive. Take off the rose-coloured glasses
and prepare to face the naked reality.

☽ ♐︎
Moon in Sagittarius

T F S S M T W T F S S M T W T F S S M T W T F S S M T W T F
1 2 3 4 5 6 7 8 9 10 11 12 13 14 15 16 17 18 19 20 21 22 23 24 25 26 27 28 29 30

JU LY

the first day
of the month
starts with the
ephemeris

☉	9º	♋
☽	12º	♐
☿	9º	♋
♀	21º	♌
♂	24º	♌
♃	9º	♉
♄℞	7º	♓
♅	22º	♉
♆℞	28º	♓
♇℞	29º	♑

MON	TUE	WED
03	04	05
10	11	12
17	18	19
24	25	26
31		

THU	FRI	SAT	SUN
		01	02
06	07	08	09
13	14	15	16
20	21	22	23
27	28	29	30

☼

☉ ☌ ☿ ♋
Sun meets Mercury in Cancer

JUL

01

SAT

A perfect day to visit the past and its origins. All
research work and archives are also favoured.

☿ ♋ ✳ ♃ ♉
Mercury in Cancer sextile Jupiter in Taurus

You may find even more ancient relics in your search. If you are in a
study phase, today is a wonderful day to complete a project or a thesis.

☉ ♋ ✳ ♃ ♉
Sun in Cancer sextile Jupiter in Taurus

A great weekend to enjoy lots of comfort and perhaps some good food! You can organize
a reunion of family or friends, at home or in a very cosy place. Remember old stories and
tell the tale of your family to the younger ones. A day to be in a home full of love!

♆ ℞ ♓
Neptune Retrograde in Pisces until 6th December

We have until the end of the year to look at our reality in a truer way. Our inspirations and intuition
gain a reality filter; it's wonderful to give even more expression to what we always dreamed.

☽ ♐
Moon in Sagittarius

☼

JUL

02

SUN

♀ ♌ □ ♅ ♉
Venus in Leo squares Uranus in Taurus

Your self-esteem may be tested today. Try
not to prove your worth to those who don't
even deserve your attention. Surprising news
could make you fall into unnecessary drama.
Beware of spending on online purchases.

☽ ♑
Moon in Capricorn

JUL
03
MON

○ ♑
Full Moon 11º Capricorn

The full Moon this month will make you look at the material achievements you have built all this year. Are you happy with your achievements in 2023? What steps do you believe you still need to climb in your life to feel fulfilled? What is being successful for you? Answer these questions and reflect on your journey so far.

JUL
04
TUE

☽ ♒
Moon in Aquarius

JUL
05
WED

☽ ≈
Moon in Aquarius

JUL
06
THU

☽ ♓
Moon in Pisces

JUL

07

FRI

☿ ♋ ✳ ♅ ♉
Mercury in Cancer sextile Uranus in Taurus

Another great weekend to take a getaway to a place in the mountains, near a lake or by the sea. Invite someone special to have a conversation whispered into your ear. Try to overcome past communication difficulties – this is a good time to explain to someone how you felt a long time ago. Overcome your shyness by talking about your emotions.

☽ ♓
Moon in Pisces

JUL

08

SAT

☽ ♈
Moon in Aries

JUL
09
SUN

☿ ♋ △ Ψ ℞ ♓
Mercury in Cancer trine Neptune Rx in Pisces

A Sunday to settle down in love! Enjoy a
pleasant Sunday with great company and good
laughs. Have lunch at a place you've always
dreamed of going, or take the opportunity to
cook an old family recipe for someone special.

◑ ♈
Last Quarter 17º Aries

Put aside your armour, drop your weapons
and reveal the real you. We are all pure
child souls, yearning to learn to LOVE! A
great idea is to put on some music and
dance like no one is watching you.

JUL
10
MON

☿ ♋ ☍ ♇ ℞ ♑
Mercury in Cancer opposite Pluto Rx in Capricorn

All the romanticism of the weekend can receive
a bucket of cold water this Monday. Maybe you
have your head in the clouds, but work demands
attention and your boss may call you in for a bit of
a tough talk. Get back on track and get to work!

♂ ♍
Mars enters Virgo until 27th August

With Mars transiting Virgo it's easier to get back to the
practical details that our work on Earth requires. Even
with your heart pounding, try to focus on getting the job
done that needs to be done, and done impeccably. Don't
do things casually or you'll have to redo them in the future.

☽ ♉
Moon in Taurus

JUL
11
TUE

☿ ♌
Mercury enters Leo until 28th July

With Mercury moving into Leo our energy changes
dramatically. We gain a fuller voice and want to speak
from our heart. Time to think about how to be even more
generous and share your brilliance and message on a
stage, with the spotlight on you. The show must begin!

☽ ♉
Moon in Taurus

JUL
12
WED

☽ ♉
Moon in Taurus

JUL
13
THU

☽ ♊
Moon in Gemini

JUL
14
FRI

☉ ♋ ✳ ♅ ♉
Sun in Cancer sextile Uranus in Taurus

As if by magick, something that happened to you in the
past can attract the attention of others and make you
recognized and valued in the present. Your story of
overcoming difficulties can inspire others to face their
own. Tell someone about something that has happened
to you but that you managed to turn around.

☽ ♊
Moon in Gemini

S S M T W T F S S M T W T F S S M T W T F S S M T W T F S S M
1 2 3 4 5 6 7 8 9 10 11 12 13 14 15 16 17 18 19 20 21 22 23 24 25 26 27 28 29 30 31

JUL
15
SAT

☽ ♋
Moon in Cancer

JUL
16
SUN

☽ ♋
Moon in Cancer

S S M T W T F S S M T W T F S S M T W T F S S M T W T F S S M
1 2 3 4 5 6 7 8 9 10 11 12 13 14 15 16 17 18 19 20 21 22 23 24 25 26 27 28 29 30 31

JUL
17
MON

☿ ♌ □ ♃ ♉
Mercury in Leo squares Jupiter in Taurus

Maybe your desire to be recognized and
valued will push you to increase the stories
and situations to boost your image. Don't
try to start a journey from the top just yet.

● ♋
New Moon 24º Cancer

New Moon in Cancer helps you to monitor how
you nurture yourself emotionally. Plant the right
seeds to gain confidence and feel that you belong
in the world. Light is born from deep within you!

JUL
18
TUE

☽ ♌
Moon in Leo

Meditation for the month of Av
Scan with your eyes from right to left

C A N C E R

JULY 17TH – 6:32PM (UTC) – 24° CANCER

Los Angeles (UTC -7) • New York (UTC -4) • London (UTC +1)
Paris (UTC +2) • Sydney (UTC +10)

SET YOUR INTENTIONS FOR THE NEXT 6 MONTHS

HOW ARE YOU GOING TO GET THERE?

Nourish	Past memories	Cook
Nutrition	Protection	Ancestral heritage
Sentimental	Take care of myself	Romance
Emotional patterns	Caring for your home	Intuition

JUL
19
WED

☽ ♌
Moon in Leo

JUL
20
THU

☉ ♋ △ ♆ ℞ ♓
Sun in Cancer trine Neptune Rx in Pisces

Day of plenty of creativity and turning memories into art! All work involving effective writing gains prominence. Write a letter or postcard to someone who is far away from you at this time.

♂ ♍ ☍ ♄ ℞ ♓
Mars in Virgo opposite Saturn Rx in Pisces

Imagination and dreams take you far but we need to have our feet firmly on the ground for the manifestation to happen. Today is the day to align the cards between your visions of the world and the real world. Put everything in lists!

☽ ♍
Moon in Virgo

JUL
21
FRI

☉ ♋ ♂ ♇ ℞ ♑
Sun in Cancer opposite Pluto Rx in Capricorn

Power and intensity are today's central themes. Whether you are the one exercising or the one suffering, try not to get stuck in any complicated situation that makes you even more insecure. A demanding Friday, as despite your willpower, your superiors challenge you to be more practical and develop a more realistic view of the future.

☽ ♍
Moon in Virgo

JUL
22
SAT

♀ St ℞ ♌
Venus Stations Retrograde 28º Leo

Venus stations for its retrogradation in Leo. Time to look in the mirror and see yourself without filters!

☉ ♌
Sun enters Leo

On the same day, the Sun enters Leo and proposes a real party! Perhaps with the help of Venus, this could be a more democratic and generous celebration than in recent years. We will see!

LEO

July 23rd / 01:50am (UTC)

△
FIRE

☉
SUN

LEO

MODE Fixed   **ELEMENT** Fire   **RULING PLANET** Sun

CRYSTAL Ruby   **BACH FLOWER REMEDY** Vervain

PRINCIPLE Positive   **OPPOSITE SIGN** Aquarius

LEO AND SIGNS IN LOVE

Aries	♥ ♥ ♥ ♥ ♡	Libra	♥ ♥ ♥ ♥ ♡
Taurus	♥ ♥ ♥ ♡ ♡	Scorpio	♥ ♡ ♡ ♡ ♡
Gemini	♥ ♥ ♥ ♥ ♡	Sagittarius	♥ ♥ ♥ ♥ ♥
Cancer	♥ ♥ ♡ ♡ ♡	Capricorn	♥ ♥ ♡ ♡ ♡
Leo	♥ ♥ ♥ ♡ ♡	Aquarius	♥ ♥ ♥ ♥ ♥
Virgo	♥ ♥ ♡ ♡ ♡	Pisces	♥ ♡ ♡ ♡ ♡

MANTRA I want   **POWER** Magnetism

KEYWORD Creating   **ANATOMY** Heart, Back, Spine

LIGHT	SHADOW
Self-assertive	Dramatic
Idealistic	Worried about status
Ambitious	Proud
Creative	Arrogant
Majestic	Afraid of ridicule
Generous	Vain
Romantic	Pretentious
Optimistic	Autocratic
Self-confident	Centre of attention

♀ ℞ ♌
Venus Retrograde in Leo until 3rd September

JUL
23
SUN

Venus retrogrades for 40 days every one and a half years. This time we will review our talents and reignite our internal flame so that we can share our light with the world in a more genuine way. Look at yourself and listen to what makes your heart beat with the strength of a lion!

☿ ♌ □ ♅ ♉
Mercury in Leo squares Uranus in Taurus

The first lesson of this review proposed by Venus is: be careful with what you exclude from your life because you think it does not shine as brightly as you do. Despite your magnificent desires, beware of impulsiveness.

☽ ♎
Moon in Libra

JUL
24
MON

☽ ♎
Moon in Libra

JUL
25
TUE

◑ ♏
First Quarter 2º Scorpio

A good time to strengthen your objective
and determined side even more. Work on
your insecurities, and your self-esteem
will flourish from within your soul. Make
an investment in yourself today.

JUL
26
WED

☽ ♏
Moon in Scorpio

JUL

27

THU

☿ ♂ ♀ ℞ ♌
Mercury meets Venus Rx in Leo

Someone may come to repay an old debt, or have a
conversation that should have happened a long time
ago. You may come to value something you once
despised. Your grace and charm will come back
into play, so take advantage of it.

☽ ♐
Moon in Sagittarius

JUL

28

FRI

☿ ♍
Mercury enters Virgo until 4th October (will retrograde)

Mercury enters another one of its houses, now to look with
very attentive eyes at the smallest details and to analyse
how we communicate in relationships. This is a time to be
more critical and to be attached to small things. Take the
opportunity to focus your attention on what really matters.

☽ ♐
Moon in Sagittarius

JUL
29
SAT

☽ ♐
Moon in Sagittarius

JUL
30
SUN

☽ ♑
Moon in Capricorn

JUL
31
MON

☽ ♑
Moon in Capricorn

AUGUST

the first day
of the month
starts with the
ephemeris

☉	9º	♌
☽	5º	♒
☿	4º	♍
♀ᴿ	27º	♌
♂	13º	♍
♃	14º	♉
♄ᴿ	6º	♓
♅	23º	♉
♆ᴿ	27º	♓
♇ᴿ	29º	♑

MON	TUE	WED
	01	02
07	08	09
14	15	16
21	22	23
28	29	30

THU	FRI	SAT	SUN
03	04	05	06
10	11	12	13
17	18	19	20
24	25	26	27
31			

AUG

01

TUE

♂ ♍ △ ♃ ♉
Mars in Virgo trine Jupiter in Taurus

Energy is focused and directed toward great
achievements. Today is an excellent day to receive
a significant award for your studies and dedication.
A day to feel proud with a pure and warm heart.

☿ ♍ ☍ ♄ ℞ ♓
Mercury in Virgo opposite Saturn Rx in Pisces

It is time to celebrate efforts but in the midst of it
all you may feel worried or a little regretful about
some mistakes. Don't focus on what went wrong;
instead learn so you can get it right in the future.

○ ♒
Full Moon 9º Aquarius

Valentine's Full Moon for Kabbalah! Tu B'av is when we
feel that our love for others is so great that it overcomes
any difference. Women wear white and go dancing to meet
their life partners. Time to share your light with the world!

AUG

02

WED

☽ ♒
Moon in Aquarius

AUG
03
THU

☽ ♓
Moon in Pisces

AUG
04
FRI

☽ ♓
Moon in Pisces

☆

AUG
05
SAT

☽ ♈
Moon in Aries

☆

AUG
06
SUN

☉ ♌ □ ♃ ♉
Sun in Leo squares Jupiter in Taurus

You are ready to receive everything the
Universe wants to give you, but don't risk
too much by showing more than you really
are. A well-measured self-esteem is the
key you need to reach even higher levels.

☽ ♈
Moon in Aries

AUG

07

MON

☽ ♉
Moon in Taurus

AUG

08

TUE

◑ ♉
Last Quarter 15º Taurus

Something you valued some time ago is loses
strength and is no longer important to you. to. A
good time for you to say goodbye to an old way of
trusting yourself and make room for the new.

AUG
09
WED

♀ ℞ ♌ □ ♅ ♉
Venus Rx in Leo squares Uranus in Taurus
(2nd – 2nd July)

Old loves could resurface and leave you in
doubt. There is a need to be valued again, but
you may be demanding too much of people and
offering too little. Inconsistency is your greatest
enemy at this time.

☿ ♍ △ ♃ ♉
Mercury in Virgo trine Jupiter in Taurus

You have all the tools you need to move your
destiny in the way that suits you. But too much
focus on small things wastes your time and
prevents you from moving forward. Deliver
the work without excesses, and move on!

☽ ♊
Moon in Gemini

AUG
10
THU

☽ ♊
Moon in Gemini

AUG
11
FRI

☽ ♋
Moon in Cancer

AUG
12
SAT

☽ ♋
Moon in Cancer

AUG
13
SUN

☉ ♂ ♀ ℞ ♌
Sun meets Venus Rx in Leo

This is a season when you will be receiving
the blessings of the Universe that you should
have received long ago. Or you are wanting
to be rewarded for a noble attitude from the
past. Beware of excessive self-indulgence
and spending on superfluous things.

☽ ♋
Moon in Cancer

AUG
14
MON

☽ ♌
Moon in Leo

Meditation for the month of Elul
Scan with your eyes from right to left

L E O

AUGUST 16TH – 9:38AM (UTC) – 23° LEO
Los Angeles (UTC -7) • New York (UTC -4) • London (UTC +1)
Paris (UTC +2) • Sydney (UTC +10)

SET YOUR INTENTIONS FOR THE NEXT 6 MONTHS

HOW ARE YOU GOING TO GET THERE?

Being queen or king	Proud of yourself	Hair care
Shine with the heart	Generosity	Power
Your talents	Self-confidence	Self-expression
Creative projects	Vanity	Individuality

AUG

15

TUE

☉ ♌ □ ⛢ ♉
Sun in Leo squares Uranus in Taurus

Things are changing: life is proposing a new
way of looking at and caring for yourself. Accept
this moment of transformation and even seek it
out – this increases your chances of making the
best of this financially unstable period.

☽ ♌
Moon in Leo

AUG

16

WED

♂ ♍ △ ⛢ ♉
Mars in Virgo trine Uranus in Taurus

After accepting the changes, the Universe will surprise you by
bringing abundant opportunities to work and to offer the world
your best services. Trust your sixth sense to guide you to accept
the best experiences. Your effort will lead you to success.

● ♌
New Moon 23º Leo

New Moon in Leo, activating old childhood dreams. What did you
say you wanted to be when you grew up? Does what you do today
relate in any way to what you dreamed of doing? What is the most
beautiful and enlightened thing you would like to share with the
world? Plant seeds of courage and your light will shine naturally.

AUG
17
THU

☽ ♍
Moon in Virgo

AUG
18
FRI

☽ ♍
Moon in Virgo

T W T F S S M T W T F S S M T W T F S S M T W T F S S M T W T
1 2 3 4 5 6 7 8 9 10 11 12 13 14 15 16 17 18 19 20 21 22 23 24 25 26 27 28 29 30 31

AUG
19
SAT

☽ ♎
Moon in Libra

AUG
20
SUN

☽ ♎
Moon in Libra

AUG
21
MON

☽ ♏
Moon in Scorpio

AUG
22
TUE

♀ ℞ ♌ □ ♃ ♉
Venus Rx in Leo squares Jupiter in Taurus
(2nd – 2nd July)

Venus is again having a conversation with Jupiter, so you
should think more about whether you are going overboard
with spending or how you wish to show off. Set limits again
and check once more that you are not deluding yourself and
fantasizing about your desires in order not to
feel guilty.

♂ ♍ ☍ ♆ ℞ ♓
Mars in Virgo opposite Neptune Rx in Pisces

Confusion in finances. Something that should have rules is
completely out of control. Large undertakings can divert you
from what was planned. Take a deep breath and try to be
patient with yourself and the situation. See this as a lesson.

☽ ♏
Moon in Scorpio

T W T F S S M T W T F S S M T W T F S S M T W T F S S M T W T
1 2 3 4 5 6 7 8 9 10 11 12 13 14 15 16 17 18 19 20 21 22 23 24 25 26 27 28 29 30 31

VIRGO

August 23rd / 09:01am (UTC)

EARTH

MERCURY

VIRGO

MODE Mutable　**ELEMENT** Earth　**RULING PLANET** Mercury

CRISTAL Peridot　**BACH FLOWER REMEDY** Centaury

PRINCIPLE Negative　**OPPOSITE SIGN** Pisces

VIRGO AND SIGNS IN LOVE

Aries	♥ ♥ ♥ ♡ ♡	Libra	♥ ♥ ♥ ♡ ♡
Taurus	♥ ♥ ♥ ♥ ♥	Scorpio	♥ ♥ ♥ ♥ ♡
Gemini	♥ ♥ ♡ ♡ ♡	Sagittarius	♥ ♡ ♡ ♡ ♡
Cancer	♥ ♥ ♥ ♥ ♡	Capricorn	♥ ♥ ♥ ♥ ♡
Leo	♥ ♥ ♡ ♡ ♡	Aquarius	♥ ♡ ♡ ♡ ♡
Virgo	♥ ♥ ♥ ♡ ♡	Pisces	♥ ♥ ♥ ♥ ♥

MANTRA I analyse　**POWER** Practicality

KEYWORD Dedication　**ANATOMY** Intestines, Liver, Vesicle, Lower Plexus

LIGHT	SHADOW
Diligent	Critical
Scientific	Stingy
Methodical	Melancholic
Discerning	Egocentric
Fact-finding	Afraid of disease and poverty
Demanding	Difficult to please
Clean	Pedantic
Pursuit of perfection	Skeptical

AUG
23
WED

⊙ ♍
Sun enters Virgo

The Sun enters Virgo and we commit ourselves
to cleanse and purify our past, to put order in
the house, to get rid of what is no longer useful.
We have a month to forgive ourselves and to
prepare ourselves to begin another stage in the
wheel of the year and of the seasons.

☿ St ℞ ♍
Mercury Stations Retrograde (Rx) in 21º Virgo

Right around the time of the entrance of the Sun in
Virgo, its ruler Mercury decides to stop and rethink
your planning and your strategy up to this point.
Don't decide anything important in the next 21 days.

☿ ℞ ♍
Mercury Rx in Virgo until 15th September

AUG
24
THU

It's time to take a critical look at everything that has been
preventing us from being even better and serving the world in
the most satisfactory way. After so much exaggeration, it's time
to put the ego back in your pocket and work more on humility.

♂ ♍ △ ♇ ℞ ♑
Mars in Virgo trine Pluto Rx in Capricorn

The change of energy in the Cosmos is already reflected in our
daily life, and now we can feel the power we have when we put
some restrictions on ourselves. The contained energy can easily be
channelled to reach the top of the mountain! Let's go that way now.

◐ ♐
First Quarter 1º Sagittarius

Our will to find the answers we have always been searching for grows
even more. We are following our new life philosophy and fitting into a
new path that is much more aligned with our life purpose. Keep going!

AUG
25
FRI

☽ ♐
Moon in Sagittarius

AUG
26
SAT

☽ ♑
Moon in Capricorn

T W T F S S M T W T F S S M T W T F S S M T W T F S S M T W T
1 2 3 4 5 6 7 8 9 10 11 12 13 14 15 16 17 18 19 20 21 22 23 24 25 26 27 28 29 30 31

AUG
27
SUN

☉ ♍ ☍ ♄ ℞ ♓
Sun in Virgo opposite Saturn Rx in Pisces

This aspect will indicate all the answers to the questions
you've been asking yourself and showing you the award
you deserve – losses or profits – all according to your past
actions. It could be an extremely rewarding time or it could
teach you a hard lesson. Low energy in the air, just rest.

♂ ♎
Mars enters Libra until 12th October

Mars in Libra learns to balance attitudes. We were very
exaggerated recently, and suddenly the energy of the Universe
asks us to control everything to the maximum. The best way is
always the harmony between the opposites. Watch yourself and
be delicate and elegant in the way you act in the coming days.

☽ ♒
Moon in Aquarius

AUG
28
MON

♅ St ℞ ♉
Uranus Stations Retrograde (Rx) in 23º Taurus

The second half of the year is always
accompanied by the retrogradation
of Uranus. Time to take a break from
technological advances and take care
of what has already been done.

☽ ♒
Moon in Aquarius

AUG
29
TUE

♅ ℞ ♉
Uranus Rx in Taurus until 27th January 2024

Between now and next year, do not try to innovate too much
on your social networks, do not schedule any big launch.
Instead, review your profiles, plan a new visual identity,
a new sales and marketing strategy, but leave everything
on standby for now. Don't invest in new equipment either:
wait for the turn of the year for new acquisitions.

☽ ♒
Moon in Aquarius

AUG
30
WED

○ ♓
Full Moon 7º Pisces

Romantic and dreamy Full Moon! What was
the mystical and spiritual ideal you wished
to achieve in 2023? What seeds of love and
giving did you promise to plant and spread in
March this year? Review your list of intentions
and celebrate the first advances. Today you
consolidate one of your dreams in the world!

AUG
31
THU

☽ ♓
Moon in Pisces

SEP TEM BER

MON	TUE	WED
04	05	06
11	12	13
18	19	20
25	26	27

the first day
of the month
starts with the
ephemeris

☉ 8º ♍

☽ 29º ♓

☿℞ 19º ♍

♀℞ 12º ♌

♂ 3º ♎

♃ 16º ♉

♄℞ 3º ♓

♅℞ 23º ♉

♆℞ 27º ♓

♇℞ 28º ♑

THU	FRI	SAT	SUN
	01	02	03
07	08	09	10
14	15	16	17
21	22	23	24
28	29	30	

SEP

01

FRI

☽ ♈
Moon in Aries

SEP

02

SAT

☽ ♈
Moon in Aries

F S S M T W T F S S M T W T F S S M T W T F S S M T W T F S
1 2 3 4 5 6 7 8 9 10 11 12 13 14 15 16 17 18 19 20 21 22 23 24 25 26 27 28 29 30

SEP

03

SUN

♀ St D ♌
Venus St Direct in 12º Leo

Venus prepares to awaken, glorious after a
sleep of more than 40 days, revisiting your
internal organs and polishing your inner glow.
Tomorrow we feel even more powerful!

☽ ♉
Moon in Taurus

♀ D ♌
Venus Direct in Leo

We start the week with glamorous, refreshed and energized Venus direct
in the sign of Leo. Those were hard lessons in self-esteem that led us to
keep the ego a little more under control. Now, yes, we can shine without
overshadowing or taking merit away from anyone. This is how we progress.

SEP

04

MON

☿ ℞ ♍ △ ♃ ♉
Mercury Rx in Virgo trine Jupiter in Taurus (2nd – 9th August)

The second conversation of these two, now with Mercury Rx and Jupiter
about to review their opinions too. The tools are at your disposal. Just review
the way you are going to use them: reassemble your strategy, redo the plans.

♃ St ℞ ♉
Jupiter Stations Retrograde (Rx) in 15º Taurus

Jupiter is preparing to expand our inner confidence now. Time to review our
values, the basis of our security and everything that keeps us steady on the path.

☽ ♉
Moon in Taurus

SEP
05
TUE

♃ ℞ ♉
Jupiter Rx in Taurus until 30th December

We have almost four months to retrace our route to a
new internal resolution. Creating new self-affirmations
is a great exercise. Say to yourself in the mirror: "I
have the internal protection and strength that allow
me to continue firmly on my path of evolution. This
is the only way I can inspire others around me!"

☽ ♊
Moon in Gemini

SEP
06
WED

☉ ♂ ☿ ℞ ♍
Sun meets Mercury Rx in Virgo

Halfway along the path, Mercury begins to see
its own internal trap. Self-criticism is very high
and it is not good to continue sabotaging yourself.
Ask forgiveness for the internal dialogue of the
last months and clear your mind with meditation.
Make room for a new way of analysing your life.

◑ ♊
Last Quarter 14º Gemini

Leave procrastination, daydreaming and lack
of focus aside. Commit yourself even more to
what you want to manifest. We are arriving in
a new season, we need to leave extra baggage
behind. Overthinking is not at all sexy.

SEP
07
THU

☽ ♊
Moon in Gemini

SEP
08
FRI

☉ ♍ △ ♃ ℞ ♉
Sun in Virgo trine Jupiter Rx in Taurus

We begin to see a light at the end of the tunnel. We seem to feel an enthusiasm of a kind we haven't felt in a long time. All this is a consequence of the internal work you've been doing, balancing self-criticism and self-esteem. Keep looking at yourself.

☽ ♋
Moon in Cancer

SEP
09
SAT

☽ ♋
Moon in Cancer

✩

SEP
10
SUN

☽ ♌
Moon in Leo

SEP

11

MON

☽ ♌
Moon in Leo

SEP

12

TUE

☽ ♌
Moon in Leo

SEP
13
WED

☽ ♍
Moon in Virgo

SEP
14
THU

● ♍
New Moon 21º Virgo

New Moon in Virgo cleansing and purifying our judgements so that
we can be freer and even more at the service of a better world. A
great time to review your routines, do a medical checkup, to return
to a more balanced diet, do an energetic and physical detox. Set
your intentions to be even healthier in the coming months.

Meditation for the month of Tishrei
Scan with your eyes from right to left

VIRGO

SEPTEMBER 15TH — 1:40AM (UTC) — 21° VIRGO

Los Angeles (UTC -7) • New York (UTC -4) • London (UTC +1)
Paris (UTC +2) • Sydney (UTC +10)

SET YOUR INTENTIONS FOR THE NEXT 6 MONTHS

_____

_____

_____

_____

_____

HOW ARE YOU GOING TO GET THERE?

_____

_____

_____

_____

_____

Organize routines	Patience	Attention to detail
Clean environments	Health checks	My body, my rules
Efficiency	Care for your body	Delicacy
Analyse	Balancing control	Forgiveness

☿ St D ♍
Mercury St Direct in 8º Virgo

Now with Mercury waking up from retrograde, we can analyse our intentions in a clearer way. Green light for all the agreements that were waiting for our decision. Organize the office, tidy up all the paperwork and commit to your destiny this week.

☉ ♍ △ ♅ ℞ ♉
Sun in Virgo trine Uranus Rx in Taurus

A good Friday to receive even more insights and have confirmation that you are on the right track! You feel the changes coming and you are now fully open and willing to face them. This is movement the Universe wants you to make, expanding toward positive personal growth! Good for you!

☽ ♎
Moon in Libra

☿ D ♍
Mercury Direct in Virgo

Mercury direct on Saturday asks you to have that conversation you've been putting off because you're not feeling totally confident. Be clear and honest with people; ask for forgiveness if you need it, as misunderstandings are in the past and you want and deserve to move on!

☽ ♎
Moon in Libra

SEP
17
SUN

♀ ♌ □ ♃ ℞ ♉
Venus in Leo squares Jupiter Rx in Taurus
(3x – 11th June / 22th August)

After the hard lessons in self-esteem, Venus is now
ready to receive her reward. More self-contained
and in control of your worth, you would be well
advised to save your resources for a big long-term
investment rather than gamble it all on instant
gratification. The measure of how much you are
valued depends on how much you value yourself.

☽ ♎
Moon in Libra

SEP
18
MON

☽ ♏
Moon in Scorpio

SEP

19

TUE

☉ ♍ ☍ ♆ ℞ ♓
Sun in Virgo opposite Neptune Rx in Pisces

Much of what you are seeing now is just the opposite of what it seems, even though you already have a better understanding of the whole scenario in front of you. Try meditating with your true intentions – even your dreams can bring you more insights and clarity. Trust your intuition.

☽ ♏
Moon in Scorpio

SEP

20

WED

☽ ♐
Moon in Sagittarius

SEP
21
THU

☉ ♍ △ ♇ ℞ ♑
Sun in Virgo trine Pluto Rx in Capricorn

Just before the Autumn Equinox we realize our
efforts so far and access our power to manifest
exactly what we deserve. Have determination to
transform your personal and professional lives,
make contact with people who are also manifested
like you. This will ease your path toward success.

☽ ♐
Moon in Sagittarius

SEP
22
FRI

◑ ♐
First Quarter 29º Sagittarius

A Friday of agitated mind and body, great for
embarking on an adventure in nature. We are more
psychic and mediumic, so being with your feet in
the grass and with friends around a campfire may
be the best choice. Grow your intention to focus on
a study that has been catching your attention lately.

F S S M T W T F S S M T W T F S S M T W T F S S M T W T F S
1 2 3 4 5 6 7 8 9 10 11 12 13 14 15 16 17 18 19 20 21 22 23 24 25 26 27 28 29 30

LIBRA

September 23rd / 06:50am (UTC)

△

AIR

♀

VENUS

LIBRA

MODE Cardinal	**ELEMENT** Air	**RULING PLANET** Venus

CRYSTAL Sapphire   **BACH FLOWER REMEDY** Scleranthus

PRINCIPLE Positive   **OPPOSITE SIGN** Aries

LIBRA AND SIGNS IN LOVE

Aries	♥ ♥ ♥ ♥ ♡	Libra	♥ ♥ ♥ ♥ ♡
Taurus	♥ ♥ ♥ ♡ ♡	Scorpio	♥ ♡ ♡ ♡ ♡
Gemini	♥ ♥ ♥ ♥ ♥	Sagittarius	♥ ♥ ♡ ♡ ♡
Cancer	♥ ♥ ♥ ♡ ♡	Capricorn	♥ ♥ ♥ ♥ ♡
Leo	♥ ♥ ♥ ♥ ♡	Aquarius	♥ ♥ ♡ ♡ ♡
Virgo	♥ ♥ ♥ ♡ ♡	Pisces	♥ ♥ ♥ ♥ ♡

MANTRA I balance   **POWER** Harmony

KEYWORD Relating   **ANATOMY** Kidneys, Appendix, Lumbar, Adrenal glands

LIGHT	SHADOW
Cooperative	Fickle
Persuasive	Apathetic
Refined	Conniving
Impartial	Peace at any price
Artistic	Grumpy
Diplomatic	Indecisive
Sociable	Easily discouraged

SEP

23

SAT

☉ ♎
Sun enters Libra
Fall Equinox – North Hemisphere
Lammas Festival

The Sun enters Libra and we balance our internal energies.
This is the day when both hemispheres receive the same
amount of light and darkness, so seek to do the same. Try to
moderate your moods and find a middle point between what
you want and what others require from you. A good Saturday
for creating something beautiful and listening to great music.

☽ ♑
Moon in Capricorn

SEP

24

SUN

☽ ♒
Moon in Aquarius

SEP
25
MON

☿ ♍ △ ♃ ℞ ♉
Mercury in Virgo trine Jupiter Rx in Taurus
(3rd – 9th Aug/4th Sept)

Mercury and Jupiter converse for the third
time and are now more centred and aware of
their powers. Concentration on achieving your
goals is total now, so don't waste time! Good
for writing, journalism, publications, distance
learning and contact with foreign countries.

☽ ♒
Moon in Aquarius

SEP
26
TUE

☽ ♓
Moon in Pisces

SEP
27
WED

☽ ♓
Moon in Pisces

SEP
28
THU

☽ ♈
Moon in Aries

SEP
29
FRI

♀ ♌ □ ♅ ℞ ♉
Venus in Leo squares Uranus Rx in Taurus
(3rd – 2nd July / 9th August)

More prepared than before, Venus now reaps the rewards
for the lessons in self-esteem and humility she has learned
since July! Once again, unexpected love could arise, but
now you know how to take advantage of the right moment
and invest the energy in a way that doesn't feel damaging!
Allow yourself to live a momentary passion!

○ ♈
Full Moon 6º Aries

At Full Moon we celebrate a new personality. Whatever
you planted on 19 April at the New Moon Eclipse is
now a reality. How have you transformed since then?
What was your great accomplishment in that time?

SEP
30
SAT

☿ ♍ △ ♅ ℞ ♉
Mercury in Virgo trine Uranus Rx in Taurus

It's Saturday but your geniality is in a high gear, and you have
the opportunity to stand out for your uniqueness. Maybe a
piece of work will gain recognition on social media, or even
something that unintentionally makes you go viral among
groups of friends. Great for launching a new trend, whether in
teaching, literature, the way you express yourself or the arts.

☽ ♉
Moon in Taurus

OC TO BER

the first day
of the month
starts with the
ephemeris

☉	8º	♎
☽	6º	♉
☿	23º	♍
♀	24º	♌
♂	22º	♎
♃ᴿ	14º	♉
♄ᴿ	1º	♓
♅ᴿ	23º	♉
♆ᴿ	26º	♓
♇ᴿ	28º	♑

MON	TUE	WED
02	03	04
09	10	11
16	17	18
23	24	25
30	31	

THU	FRI	SAT	SUN
			01
05	06	07	08
12	13	14	15
19	20	21	22
26	27	28	29

OCT

01

SUN

☽ ♉
Moon in Taurus

OCT

02

MON

☿ ♍ ☍ ♆ ℞ ♓
Mercury in Virgo opposite Neptune Rx in Pisces

We can daydream today, or it will just be another dispersed Monday. Great for all jobs that don't require attention. If channelled well, this energy can create beautiful artwork. Tomorrow you have a meeting with someone important, so set aside some time to start getting your feet back on the ground.

☽ ♉
Moon in Taurus

OCT
03
TUE

☿ ♍ △ ♇ ℞ ♑
Mercury in Virgo trine Pluto in Capricorn

After a day with our heads in the clouds, we are more
focused and ready to have important meetings. Your
power of persuasion is stronger today, and you can
convince anyone of your bolder ideas and dreams.

☽ ♊
Moon in Gemini

OCT
04
WED

☿ ♎
Mercury enters Libra until 22nd October

Mercury enters Libra to help us measure the level
of dedication and surrender in relationships. A good
time to make a successful partnership in love or
business. Count on outside help to deepen your
studies, set up a duo and continue your progress.

☽ ♊
Moon in Gemini

S M T W T F S S M T W T F S S M T W T F S S M T W T F S S M T
1 2 3 4 5 6 7 8 9 10 11 12 13 **14 15** 16 17 18 19 20 **21 22** 23 24 25 26 27 **28 29** 30 31

OCT
05
THU

☽ ♋
Moon in Cancer

OCT
06
FRI

☾ ♋
Last Quarter 13º Cancer

Friday is a little nostalgic – good to let go of old
attachments or memories of pain. Rewrite your story by
pulling yourself out of victimhood and into the shoes of
the protagonist. Let go of any unresolved stories from
the past and move on more lightly toward your future.

OCT
07
SAT

☽ ♌
Moon in Leo

OCT
08
SUN

♂ ♎ ☐ ♇ ℞ ♑
Mars in Libra squares Pluto Rx in Capricorn

Sunday of important aspects. Our diplomacy will be in demand
when someone with more power than us tries to destabilize us. In
relationships, beware of power games, or of giving too much of your
energy to those who only want to take advantage of your position.

♀ ♍
Venus enters Virgo until 8th November

After a possible clash, Venus moves on to Virgo to examine all your
desires thoroughly. Beware of over-analysing your values and emotions
or you could end up exterminating any lighter, more spontaneous
attitude. You should rather study your professional inclinations, and
your desires at work, so that you don't misjudge your feelings.

☽ ♌
Moon in Leo

OCT
09
MON

☽ ♌
Moon in Leo

OCT
10
TUE

♀ ♍ ☍ ♄ ℞ ♓
Venus in Virgo opposite Saturn Rx in Pisces

A certain discouragement could overwhelm
you as Venus in Virgo does not give us peace
and quiet, and the tendency is to sacrifice
pleasures in the name of service, of work.
Try to soften the tendency to be so rigid with
your emotions, let go of the control a little and
learn to flow a little more in relationships.

♇ St D ♑
Pluto St Direct in 27º Capricorn

On the same day Pluto begins its ascent
from our depths, to the surface. To access
our darkest treasures we had to go deep
into our shadows. It is by facing and
mastering our demons that we are able to
light up even more, and more strongly.

☽ ♍
Moon in Virgo

OCT
11
WED

♇ ♀ ♑
Pluto Direct in Capricorn

Pluto puts us back on the track of life. We now have the direction and are the captains of our own ship. With the entrance of Mars in Scorpio we gain even more intensity and we are ready to reach the top of our journey.

☽ ♍
Moon in Virgo

OCT
12
THU

♂ ♏
Mars enters Scorpio until 24th November

Mars enters the sign when we become even more confident and determined. Nothing can stop us from getting where we want to go. Planning and strategy are very important at this time, as well as hard work so we can achieve a lot. Stay calm and observe before you act.

☽ ♎
Moon in Libra

OCT
13
FRI

♂ ♏ △ ♄ ℞ ♓
Mars in Scorpio trine Saturn Rx in Pisces

Mars enters the sign where we become even
more confident and determined. Nothing can
stop us from getting where we want. Planning
and strategy are important in this very significant
moment. Work hard so we can conquer many
things. Stay calm and observe before acting.

☽ ♎
Moon in Libra

OCT
14
SAT

● ♎
New Moon Annular Eclipse 21º Libra

Saturday of eclipsing a former identity, leaving an old
aggressiveness by the wayside because it is no longer
necessary to show your weapons. You have the strength
and fortitude to rebuild your new personality, more open to
new ideas, in search of your self-realization. What else is
motivating you now? What is the big risk you want to take in
the next six months? Plant the seeds and develop patience.

Meditation for the month of Cheshvan
Scan with your eyes from right to left

L I B R A

OCTOBER 14TH – 5:55PM (UTC) – 21° LIBRA ECLIPSE ANNULAR
Los Angeles (UTC -7) • New York (UTC -4) • London (UTC +1) • Paris (UTC +2) • Sydney (UTC +10)

SET YOUR INTENTIONS FOR THE NEXT 6 MONTHS

HOW ARE YOU GOING TO GET THERE?

Relationships	Creating harmony	Give your opinion
Partnerships	Perfectionism	Justice and honesty
Commitment	Visual aesthetics	Elegance
Reconciliation	Your own voice	Charm

OCT

15

SUN

☽ ♏
Moon in Scorpio

OCT

16

MON

☽ ♏
Moon in Scorpio

OCT
17
TUE

☽ ♐
Moon in Sagittarius

OCT
18
WED

☽ ♐
Moon in Sagittarius

OCT
19
THU

☽ ♑
Moon in Capricorn

OCT
20
FRI

☉ ☌ ☿ ♎
Sun meets Mercury in Libra

After the Eclipse we are more willing to relate in a more balanced way. Our new personality calls for new friendships. An excellent day to attend social events, go to an art exhibition, music, a party with interesting people. Be open to the new!

☿ ♎ □ ♇ ♑
Mercury in Libra squares Pluto in Capricorn

With this combination, your power of persuasion is above the normal. Just be careful not to take unnecessary risks, not to impress by talking about controversial or extreme subjects. The ideal mental balance is to be sought at this time.

☽ ♑
Moon in Capricorn

S M T W T F S S M T W T F S S M T W T F S S M T W T F S S M T
1 2 3 4 5 6 7 8 9 10 11 12 13 14 15 16 17 18 19 20 21 22 23 24 25 26 27 28 29 30 31

OCT
21
SAT

☉ ♎ □ ♇ ♑
Sun in Libra squares Pluto in Capricorn

After yesterday's events, a certain arrogance could arise,
or you could be very pleased with the achievements
and conversations of the last few days. Today you show
yourself in a not-so-true way – good for performances,
role-playing and theatre. Try to put ego aside and seek
more constructive channels for this energy.

☽ ♑
Moon in Capricorn

OCT
22
SUN

♀ ♍ △ ♃ Rx ♉
Venus in Virgo trine Jupiter Rx in Taurus

Busy Sunday. Venus wants to be more recognized at work – she is working so hard, after all!
Your high ideals will be admired. Take advantage of Sunday to plan your next career steps.

☿ ♏
Mercury enters Scorpio until 10th November

With this shift of energy, it's easy to focus on strategy going forward. Mercury turns into a
real detective in Scorpio: whatever is obstructing your path will be illuminated now.

☿ ♏ △ ♄ Rx ♓
Mercury in Scorpio trine Saturn Rx in Pisces

Maximum concentration on your plans and dreams. Go back as many times as necessary
to what you wanted to live this year, your list of priorities and how you plan to get there!

◑ ♑
First Quarter 28º Capricorn

Another transit that pushes you to the top of the mountain. You know it won't be easy to
get there, but today you have the chance to give your needs and ambitions an extra push.

SCORPIO

October 23rd / 4:21pm (UTC)

WATER

PLUTO

SCORPIO

MODE Fixed	**ELEMENT** Water	**RULING PLANET** Pluto	

CRYSTAL Tourmaline	**BACH FLOWER REMEDY** Chicory

PRINCIPLE Negative	**OPPOSITE SIGN** Taurus

SCORPIO AND SIGNS IN LOVE

Aries	♥ ♥ ♥ ♥ ♡	Libra	♥ ♡ ♡ ♡ ♡
Taurus	♥ ♥ ♥ ♥ ♥	Scorpio	♥ ♥ ♥ ♡ ♡
Gemini	♥ ♡ ♡ ♡ ♡	Sagittarius	♥ ♥ ♡ ♡ ♡
Cancer	♥ ♥ ♥ ♥ ♡	Capricorn	♥ ♥ ♥ ♡ ♡
Leo	♥ ♡ ♡ ♡ ♡	Aquarius	♥ ♥ ♡ ♡ ♡
Virgo	♥ ♥ ♥ ♥ ♡	Pisces	♥ ♥ ♥ ♥ ♥

MANTRA I desire	**POWER** Intensity

ANATOMY Reproductive system, Sexual organs, Bladder

LIGHT	SHADOW
Motivated	Vengeful
Penetrating	Temperamental
Director	Reticent
Determined	Arrogant
Scientifically curious	Sarcastic
Researcher	Suspicious
Passionate	Jealous
Conscientious	Intolerant

OCT
23
MON

☉ ♏
Sun enters Scorpio

The Sun arrives in the deep sign of Scorpio, and we
become even more firm and decisive. A stronger and
at the same time more reserved personality hangs
over us in the coming days. We are full of desires, but
we will not fulfil them with just anyone, at any time.
Have a defined target and enjoy the intensity.

☽ ♒
Moon in Aquarius

OCT
24
TUE

☉ ♏ △ ♄ ℞ ♓
Sun in Scorpio trine Saturn Rx in Pisces

Responsibility and diplomacy: a good day for an honest
conversation with some authority figure. Patience
and slow progress with your dreams and desires –
perhaps you will be recognized for past actions or
some old commitment begins to bear fruit. Learn to do
everything on your own: be a little selfish today.

☽ ♓
Moon in Pisces

☆

OCT
25
WED

☽ ♓
Moon in Pisces

☆

OCT
26
THU

☽ ♈
Moon in Aries

OCT
27
FRI

☽ ♈
Moon in Aries

OCT
28
SAT

♂ ♏ ☍ ♃ R ♉
Mars in Scorpio opposite Jupiter Rx in Taurus

A Saturday full of intensity. Calculated risks could bring you an expansion and appreciation you've long been searching for. Take time to have a good look at everything that is appearing on the horizon for you at this time.

○ ♉
Full Moon Partial Eclipse 5º Taurus

Night to celebrate all the advances and all the internal security, the valorization that you have worked so hard for in the last six months. Your self-esteem is already responding from a much more stable place and your financial life finally seems to react to your stimulation. Celebrate by delighting your senses with all that is most pleasant things in life: music, food, wine, perfume. You deserve it!

OCT
29
SUN

☿ ♏ ☍ ♃ ℞ ♉
Mercury in Scorpio opposite Jupiter Rx in Taurus

Mental agitation and many insights are coming into
your mind at the same time. Your thoughts are more
confident but you could get caught up in false hopes.
Only commit to what you can deliver and to what
is compatible with your inner safeness. Don't put
yourself in awkward situations for nothing.

☿ ♂ ♂ ♏
Mercury meets Mars in Scorpio

This encounter of Mercury and Mars can bring
trepidation and anxiety. It's possible that some
obsession may appear to signal that it's time to take a
step back. Take time to relax, dissipating this energy
in simpler mind games, video games, board games or
even reading a mystery book or an investigative series.

☽ ♉
Moon in Taurus

OCT
30
MON

☽ ♊
Moon in Gemini

OCT

31

TUE

♀ ♍ △ ♅ ℞ ♉
Venus in Virgo trine Uranus Rx in Taurus

Quite a satisfying financial period: you may
receive a proposal or a windfall. Good for playing
the lottery, money or love. Something unexpected
could surprise you today. Enjoy being surprised
without committing yourself too much.

☽ ♊
Moon in Gemini

NO VEM BER

the first day
of the month
starts with the
ephemeris

☉	8º	♏
☽	25º	♊
☿	16º	♏
♀	22º	♍
♂	14º	♏
♃ᴿ	11º	♉
♄ᴿ	0º	♓
♅ᴿ	22º	♉
♆ᴿ	25º	♓
♇	28º	♑

MON	TUE	WED
		01
06	07	08
13	14	15
20	21	22
27	28	29

THU	FRI	SAT	SUN
02	03	04	05
09	10	11	12
16	17	18	19
23	24	25	26
30			

NOV
01
WED

☽ ♋
Moon in Cancer

NOV
02
THU

☽ ♋
Moon in Cancer

W	T	F	S	S	M	T	W	T	F	S	S	M	T	W	T	F	S	S	M	T	W	T	F	S	S	M	T	W	T
1	2	3	4	5	6	7	8	9	10	11	12	13	14	15	16	17	18	19	20	21	22	23	24	25	26	27	28	29	30

☉ ♏ ☍ ♃ ℞ ♉
Sun in Scorpio opposite Jupiter Rx in Taurus

A super magnetic and sensual day; the Sun wants
to show all your inner power and Jupiter helps to
expand this enchantment even further. You may
be feeling more attractive than usual and ready to
grab any opportunity life offers you. Be happy!

♀ ♍ ☍ ♆ ℞ ♓
Venus in Virgo opposite Neptune Rx in Pisces

In the blink of an eye your insecurities seem to give
you peace and you can travel in your unconscious
just as you've always dreamed. A realistic fantasy, a
flash romance, you could be in love or just loving the
idea of having someone. Don't stay at home if you
don't want to waste this chance – allow yourself!

☽ ♋
Moon in Cancer

♄ St D ♓
Saturn St Direct in 0º Pisces

Almost in the last minutes of Pisces, Saturn wakes
up to help us take back the controls of life and make
our dreams come true. Prepare for the big decisions
and attitudes that you will have to take this week.

☿ ♏ ☍ ♅ ℞ ♉
Mercury in Scorpio opposite Uranus in Taurus

Your intuition is stronger than ever. A day to access
your innermost desires and value yourself even more.
Trust blindly in what you feel, but be careful about
what you say without thinking or respecting others.

☽ ♌
Moon in Leo

NOV
05
SUN

♄ D ♓
Saturn Direct in Pisces

Saturn is back on track, ready to make
you take great responsibilities and to
grow and build your future! Prepare
the list of tasks you need to accomplish
this week and don't skip any steps!

◑ ♌
Last Quarter 12º Leo

This Moon asks us to leave our ego aside, to
look with more humble eyes at our talents and
to put ourselves exactly where we should be.
Practise meditation and try to disconnect from
any labels you've given yourself lately.

NOV
06
MON

♀ ♍ △ ♇ ♑
Venus in Virgo trine Pluto in Capricorn

A wonderful day to present your results to
anyone who matters. A chat with the boss
about how you are delivering your work and
how you contribute to the company is a good
thing to do today. You deserve a promotion
or the pay rise you've wanted for so long.

☿ ♏ △ ♆ ℞ ♓
Mercury in Scorpio trine Neptune Rx in Pisces

Talk about values, dream about a salary that
covers all your expenses. Do your financial
planning for next year – start planning now
to reach your goal before the year ends!

☽ ♍
Moon in Virgo

NOV
07
TUE

☽ ♍
Moon in Virgo

♀ ♎
Venus enters Libra until 4th December

NOV
08
WED

Venus returns to one of its houses and our desire
to live a romance or have a successful partnership
increases! We gain a refined air and everything we
create on these days has an even more elegant touch
of beauty! Take the opportunity to treat yourself to a
lot of pampering. Buy yourself some flowers!

☿ ♏ ✳ ♇ ♑
Mercury in Scorpio sextile Pluto in Capricorn

Today's conversations can take us to the place we've
always dreamed about! Get back in touch with
someone interesting whom you met in an informal way,
but who you discovered to be someone very important,
who can present you with the right opportunities.

☽ ♍
Moon in Virgo

NOV
09
THU

☽ ♎
Moon in Libra

NOV
10
FRI

☿ ♐
Mercury enters Sagittarius until 1st December

We have 20 days to accelerate our ideals and reach the target, riding the path of evolution. We have the desire to learn everything at the same time, and our mental agitation can also make us move our body to better distribute all this fire. Focus on the intellectual activities you like the most; writing or oratory are good choices.

☿ ♐ □ ♄ ♓
Mercury in Sagittarius squares Saturn in Pisces

In this first conversation we may feel a little intimidated. Perhaps our ambition is greater than our abilities. Direct your energy toward what will be of most value in fulfilling your dreams in the future. Do one task at a time and perseverance will succeed.

☽ ♎
Moon in Libra

NOV
11
SAT

♂ ♏ ☍ ♅ ℞ ♉
Mars in Scorpio opposite Uranus Rx in Taurus

Pay maximum attention to where you put your energy. The attraction between you and another person can be 1,000 per cent, passion on fire, but evaluate very well whether you want to keep this flame for a longer time or if you want to consume all the energy at once and go on to the next one. You'll have a lot of passion waiting for you just around the corner.

☽ ♏
Moon in Scorpio

NOV
12
SUN

☽ ♏
Moon in Scorpio

NOV
13
MON

☉ ♏ ☍ ♅ ℞ ♉
Sun in Scorpio opposite Uranus Rx in Taurus

Uranus wants to make you act differently in relationships this
time. It even seems that you are managing to value and give
yourself more importance than in previous years. The New
Moon helps you to reach the right people at the right time.

● ♏
New Moon 20º Scorpio

New Moon in Scorpio, bringing emotions to the surface,
mysticism and psychicism to the fore. A good time to connect
with your oracles, seek to better understand your unconscious
through meditation or professional help. Prepare a herbal
bath, exfoliate your body, get ready to change your skin.

NOV
14
TUE

☽ ♐
Moon in Sagittarius

Meditation for the month of Kislev
Scan with your eyes from right to left

S C O R P I O

NOVEMBER 13TH — 9:27AM (UTC) — 20° SCORPIO

Los Angeles (UTC -8) • New York (UTC -5) • London (UTC +0)
Paris (UTC +1) • Sydney (UTC +11)

SET YOUR INTENTIONS FOR THE NEXT 6 MONTHS

_____

_____

_____

_____

_____

HOW ARE YOU GOING TO GET THERE?

_____

_____

_____

_____

_____

Intensity	Take power	Surrender
Transformation	Hidden places	Deep unconscious
Magnetism	Sexuality	Transmutation
End of cycle	Keep secrets	Rebirth

NOV
15
WED

☿ ♐ ⁂ ♀ ♎
Mercury in Sagittarius sextile Venus in Libra

The desire to travel the world and take part in all events, to accept all invitations. Plan a trip somewhere interesting with friends or loved ones! You can also take some courses with your partner which will bring you closer and help you to be more intimate.

☽ ♐
Moon in Sagittarius

NOV
16
THU

☽ ♑
Moon in Capricorn

NOV
17
FRI

♂ ♏ △ Ψ ℞ ♓
Mars in Scorpio trine Neptune Rx in Pisces

Love is in the air! It seems that today all your
dreams come true. A romantic night full of pleasure
and sensuality. If you are alone, get ready to
meet someone special in the coming days. Your
magnetism attracts whoever is in the same vibration.

☉ ♏ △ Ψ ℞ ♓
Sun in Scorpio trine Neptune Rx in Pisces

The Sun wants you to be a little more
mysterious this time – don't go giving away all
your treasures without first creating intimacy.
Take it easy when revealing your powers!

☽ ♑
Moon in Capricorn

NOV
18
SAT

☉ ♂ ♂ ♏
Sun meets Mars in Scorpio

A powerful day to deepen intimacy with your
partner. The energy is very strong, so if you're not
going to channel it into pleasurable things, avoid
nervousness and uncontrolled anger as much as
possible. Strong sexual energy in the air. Enjoy!

☽ ♒
Moon in Aquarius

NOV
19
SUN

☽ ♒
Moon in Aquarius

NOV
20
MON

☉ ♏ ✳ ♇ ♑
Sun in Scorpio sextile Pluto in Capricorn

A good Monday to have another important conversation
about money and the future. Nice to invest even more
in your talents and know how to impose your values.
Moderate investments are advised today!

◐ ♒
First Quarter 27º Aquarius

Further expand our desires for a better society. It's a
great time to leave patterns of behaviour behind by
replacing them with healthier habits. What could you do
today to become a better human being in the future?

W	T	F	S	S	M	T	W	T	F	S	S	M	T	W	T	F	S	S	M	T	W	T	F	S	S	M	T	W	T
1	2	3	4	5	6	7	8	9	10	11	12	13	14	15	16	17	18	19	20	21	22	23	24	25	26	27	28	29	30

NOV
21
TUE

♂ ♏ ✳ ♇ ♑
Mars in Scorpio sextile Pluto in Capricorn

Another day to show your determination and
talk about earnings and discuss your salary
with your boss. For the self-employed, it's
time to create strategies to receive even
more resources in the coming year. Have
you planned your year-end campaign yet?

☽ ♓
Moon in Pisces

NOV
22
WED

☉ ♐
Sun enters Sagittarius

We've started the fastest month of the year,
when we're about to have fun with friends, and
we want to spread our light wherever we go.
The opportunities are many and will pass in
front of us very quickly, You need total attention
just not to exaggerate the dose of optimism.

☽ ♈
Moon in Aries

SAGITTARIUS

November 22nd / 2:03pm (UTC)

△
FIRE

♃
JUPITER

SAGITTARIUS

MODE Mutable	**ELEMENT** Fire	**RULING PLANET** Jupiter

CRYSTAL Citrine   **BACH FLOWER REMEDY** Agrimonia

PRINCIPLE Positive   **OPPOSITE SIGN** Gemini

SAGITTARIUS AND SIGNS IN LOVE

Aries	♥ ♥ ♥ ♥ ♥					Libra	♥ ♥ ♡ ♡ ♡			
Taurus	♥ ♥ ♡ ♡ ♡					Scorpio	♥ ♥ ♥ ♡ ♡			
Gemini	♥ ♥ ♥ ♥ ♡					Sagittarius	♥ ♥ ♥ ♥ ♡			
Cancer	♥ ♡ ♡ ♡ ♡					Capricorn	♥ ♥ ♡ ♡ ♡			
Leo	♥ ♥ ♥ ♥ ♥					Aquarius	♥ ♥ ♥ ♥ ♡			
Virgo	♥ ♡ ♡ ♡ ♡					Pisces	♥ ♥ ♥ ♡ ♡			

MANTRA I understand   **POWER** Visualization

KEYWORD Explore   **ANATOMY** Hips, Thighs, Upper legs

LIGHT	SHADOW
Honest	Argumentative
Philosophical	Exaggerated
Free lover	Chatty
Athletic	Procrastinator
Generous	Self-indulgent
Optimistic	Brash
Fair	Impatient
Enthusiastic	Promiscuous

NOV

23

THU

⊙ ♐ □ ♄ ♓
Sun in Sagittarius squares Saturn in Pisces

Your dose of optimism will determine the success of this aspect,
which may present itself as a beautiful chance of fulfilment in
the long term, or you may find that the situation is more like
something that limits you and makes it impossible to be free. It
all depends on how involved you are with your dreams.

☽ ♈
Moon in Aries

NOV

24

FRI

♂ ♐
Mars enters Sagittarius until 4th January 2024

Our action is directed towards a more worthy ideology,
and we can change the direction of our paths with this
aspect. Take great dedication to plan where you could
spend a few days to enlarge your vision of the world and
meet new people. Next week's Full Moon amplifies the
possibilities even further and sharpens your curiosity!

☽ ♉
Moon in Taurus

W	T	F	S	S	M	T	W	T	F	S	S	M	T	W	T	F	S	S	M	T	W	T	F	S	S	M	T	W	T
1	2	3	**4**	**5**	6	7	8	9	10	**11**	**12**	13	14	15	16	17	**18**	**19**	20	21	22	23	24	**25**	**26**	27	28	29	30

NOV
25
SAT

♂ ♐ □ ♄ ♓
Mars in Sagittarius squares Saturn in Pisces

Time to put down on paper all the expenses
that a possible adventure could cost you. If
you calculate everything in advance there will
be no surprises. Put together your holiday
spreadsheet and work consistently to achieve
your goals. You deserve this transformation!

☽ ♉
Moon in Taurus

NOV
26
SUN

☽ ♊
Moon in Gemini

NOV
27
MON

☿ ♐ □ Ψ ℞ ♓
Mercury in Sagittarius squares Neptune Rx in Pisces

Dream big and dream high. This conversation makes you explore all the paths that call for your attention now – just don't decide or buy the tickets yet. Wait for a day with more concentration, to avoid losses and cancellations.

○ ♊
Full Moon 4º Gemini

This is a Full Moon that sharpens our curiosity: we want to exchange information, meet people and have fun, but we still have one month before the end of the year. So celebrate the change of perception you have achieved this year and prepare the new mindset for the next challenges!

NOV
28
TUE

☽ ♊
Moon in Gemini

NOV
29
WED

) ♋
Moon in Cancer

NOV
30
THU

) ♋
Moon in Cancer

DECEMBER

the first day
of the month
starts with the
ephemeris

☉	9º	♐
☽	28º	♋
☿	29º	♐
♀	26º	♎
♂	5º	♐
♃ ℞	7º	♉
♄	1º	♓
♅ ℞	20º	♉
♆ ℞	25º	♓
♇	28º	♑

MON	TUE	WED
04	05	06
11	12	13
18	19	20
25	26	27

THU	FRI	SAT	SUN
	01	02	03
07	08	09	10
14	15	16	17
21	22	23	24
28	29	30	31

DEC
01
FRI

☿ ♑
Mercury enters Capricorn until 23rd December (will retrograde)

December starts with the ambitious and decided mind of Mercury in Capricorn. Trace your last goals for this year and start drawing up your new chapter – what you want to build for the year to come. These plans may change as we will review them in 13 days in retrogradation. Write down everything that comes to your mind.

☽ ♌
Moon in Leo

DEC
02
SAT

☿ ♑ ⚹ ♄ ♓
Mercury in Capricorn sextile Saturn in Pisces

A good construction needs a solid plan and a dream only comes off the paper if it is structured. We encounter obstacles that help us to hone our goals further, and make us even more determined.

☽ ♌
Moon in Leo

DEC

03

SUN

♀ ♎ □ ♇ ♑
Venus in Libra squares Pluto in Capricorn

This is a time of divergences in relationships. Perhaps
each of you wants to follow a different path. Avoid
arguments, and also do not underestimate the power of
your partner. Don't get caught up in power games. Give
it a break and try not to focus on who can have more.

☽ ♌
Moon in Leo

DEC

04

MON

♀ ♏
Venus enters Scorpio until 29th December

Scorpio is not a good place for Venus to transit as the denser
energy can lead her to be very passionate. Do everything with
a great deal of intensity but pay attention to the wishes of
others, the people you relate to. Avoid major disappointments
as feelings of rejection can easily arise in this season.

☽ ♍
Moon in Virgo

DEC
05
TUE

♀ ♏ △ ♄ ♓
Venus in Scorpio trine Saturn in Pisces

A partnership with an older or wiser person
could bring you the recognition you desire so
much. Time to build your ladder to success,
with patience and depth. If you feel lonely,
channel the energy by writing, composing or by
pulling out a Tarot. Mysticism can be a perfect
ally for these moments of much questioning.

◑ ♍
Last Quarter 12º Virgo

Give up things you thought you could control.
A great time to let go of addictions and
embrace a new routine. Look for a specialist
such as a nutritionist or psychologist to help
you break a pattern.

DEC
06
WED

♆ St D ♓
Neptune St Direct in 24º Pisces

Neptune, king of the seas and illusion, is
preparing to awaken. We put the most
colourful filters back on our lives. It's
time to dream of a possible romance!

☽ ♎
Moon in Libra

DEC
07
THU

Ψ D ♓
Neptune Direct in Pisces

Neptune is the planet that connects us with
the other dimensions, all multidimensional
practices, holistic therapies, and allows us to
gain more power from now on. Take time to
meditate on what you want to live in 2024!

☽ ♎
Moon in Libra

DEC
08
FRI

☿ ♑ △ ♃ ℞ ♉
Mercury in Capricorn trine Jupiter Rx in Taurus

A good aspect for great professional
presentations, to sell your product, show
your plan to a prospective investor partner,
get a loan to carry out a project. Just be
aware of all the clauses before signing.

☽ ♎
Moon in Libra

F S S M T W T F S S M T W T F S S M T W T F S S M T W T F S S
1 2 3 4 5 6 7 8 9 10 11 12 13 14 15 16 17 18 19 20 21 22 23 24 25 26 27 28 29 30 31

☆

DEC
09
SAT

♀ ♏ ☌ ♃ ℞ ♉
Venus in Scorpio opposite Jupiter Rx in Taurus

Venus could be wanting to take you through
the valley of the shadows, where they don't
value you and you negotiate yourself too
cheaply. You'll have to be careful about
superficial love affairs or just that consuming
passion that doesn't add anything to your life.

☽ ♏
Moon in Scorpio

☆

DEC
10
SUN

☽ ♏
Moon in Scorpio

עב

ה·י·ה·ו

Meditation for the month of Tevet
Scan with your eyes from right to left

S A G I T T A R I U S

DECEMBER 12TH – 11:32PM (UTC) – 20° SAGITTARIUS

Los Angeles (UTC -8) • New York (UTC -5) • London (UTC +0)
Paris (UTC +1) • Sydney (UTC +11)

SET YOUR INTENTIONS FOR THE NEXT 6 MONTHS

HOW ARE YOU GOING TO GET THERE?

Explore the world	Spontaneity	Long studies
New directions	Search for truth	Investigation
Freedom	Physical exercises	Philosophy
Optimism	Overkill	Foreign cultures

DEC
11
MON

☿ ♑ ✳ ♀ ♏
Mercury in Capricorn sextile Venus in Scorpio

Mercury pushes Venus into the corner for a serious chat about the future. It's great to get intimately involved, but trying to get deep with someone who only wants the superficial is a losing battle. Plan well and notice what you've been valuing lately.

☽ ♐
Moon in Sagittarius

DEC
12
TUE

● ♐
New Moon 20º Sagittarius

The New Moon is opening new paths. Our search for the highest ideals gains a magnifying glass. Are you on the path you'd like to be on? Have you found what you were looking for this year? Is there an area of your life that deserves attention and needs expansion? Answer these questions and bet your chips on the best path to follow from now on.

DEC
13
WED

♀ St ℞ ♑
Mercury Stations Retrograde (Rx) in 8º Capricorn

Mercury wants to end the year reviewing your
projects and goals for 2024. A great time to get
back to planning and strategy. Write and rewrite
everything you want to manifest in the coming year.

☽ ♑
Moon in Capricorn

DEC
14
THU

♀ ℞ ♑
Mercury Rx in Capricorn until 2nd January 2024

You have 19 days to work out your plan for the next cycle
and make it even better. What are the goals you had for this
year that ended up changing course and turning out to be
something totally different? The end result only depends
on the adjustments you make now. Sit down with a blank
sheet of paper and start your divinely inspired sketch.

☽ ♑
Moon in Capricorn

DEC
15
FRI

☽ ≈
Moon in Aquarius

DEC
16
SAT

☉ ♐ □ ♆ ♓
Sun in Sagittarius squares Neptune in Pisces

A Saturday for dispersion and creativity. Don't schedule
any activities that require too much concentration. Instead,
let your imagination wander to some good music, an art
exhibition, a cultural event or just go on a relaxed trip with
friends. Benefit from an unpretentious adventure today.

☽ ≈
Moon in Aquarius

☆

DEC

17

SUN

☽ ♓
Moon in Pisces

☆

DEC

18

MON

☿ ℞ ♑ △ ♃ ℞ ♉
Mercury Rx in Capricorn trine Jupiter Rx in Taurus
(2nd – 8th December)

The past is calling you again. It could be that an old
project brings you back the recognition for which you've
been waiting for a while. A promotion at work, or some
old promise is knocking on your door again, perhaps for
the thousandth time – watch out! With that news, your
plans change once again and it's all good. Carry on.

☽ ♓
Moon in Pisces

DEC
19
TUE

◐ ♓
First Quarter 27º Pisces

A day to do charity, help others, to give your
time and attention without expecting anything
in return. Also an excellent day for all holistic
therapies: reiki, radiesthesia, meditation, yoga.
All forms of healing are enhanced by this Moon.

DEC
20
WED

☽ ♈
Moon in Aries

☆

DEC

21

THU

♀ ♏ ☌ ♅ ℞ ♉
Venus in Scorpio opposite Uranus Rx in Taurus

Another aspect that forces us to change the way we negotiate our values
in relationships. Don't accept less than you are worth; however solitary the
journey, there are non-negotiable values. Do you know what yours are?

☿ ℞ ♑ ✳ ♄ ♓
Mercury Rx in Capricorn sextile Saturn in Pisces

Mercury has a serious chat with Saturn again, to help you give even more shape
to your dreams. You could receive help, a very important contribution if you are
working on a volunteer project. A day to distribute blessings to everyone.

☉ ♑
Sun enters Capricorn
Winter Solstice – North Hemisphere
Yule Festival

The Sun enters Capricorn to prepare the land in which we will plant the seeds
of the new time! We celebrate another season in the wheel of the year, we
welcome the light that is born from us, starting from today, towards spring.

☽ ♉
Moon in Taurus

☆

DEC

22

FRI

☉ ☌ ♀ ℞ ♑
Sun meets Mercury Rx in Capricorn

The midpoint of retrogradation. We are now getting
slightly clearer idea of how we should build our
foundations, and how solid they need to be to
support the weight of our commitments. Stay strong!

☽ ♉
Moon in Taurus

CAPRICORN

December 22nd / 03:27am (UTC)

EARTH

SATURN

CAPRICORN

MODE Cardinal   **ELEMENT** Earth   **RULING SIGN** Saturn

CRYSTAL Turquoise   **BACH FLOWER REMEDY** Mimulus

PRINCIPLE Negative   **OPPOSITE SIGN** Cancer

CAPRICORN AND SIGNS IN LOVE

Aries	♥ ♡ ♡ ♡ ♡	Libra	♥ ♥ ♥ ♡ ♡
Taurus	♥ ♥ ♥ ♥ ♥	Scorpio	♥ ♥ ♡ ♡ ♡
Gemini	♥ ♥ ♡ ♡ ♡	Sagittarius	♥ ♡ ♡ ♡ ♡
Cancer	♥ ♥ ♥ ♥ ♡	Capricorn	♥ ♥ ♥ ♡ ♡
Leo	♥ ♥ ♡ ♡ ♡	Aquarius	♥ ♥ ♡ ♡ ♡
Virgo	♥ ♥ ♥ ♥ ♥	Pisces	♥ ♥ ♥ ♡ ♡

MANTRA I use   **POWER** Ambition

ANATOMY Knees, Bones, Teeth

LIGHT	SHADOW
Cautious	Selfish
Responsible	Domineering
Scrupulous	Spiteful
Professional	Fatalistic
Traditional	Conventional
Practical	Stubborn
Economical	Inhibited
Serious worker	Status seeking

DEC

23

SAT

☿ ℞ ♐
Mercury Rx goes back to Sagittarius until 13th January 2024

Mercury returns to Sagittarius as there is an inner truth that needs to be reviewed and revisited! Something that we believed to be immutable begins to transform right before our eyes! Trust that your path of evolution must go through all this metamorphosis. A new being will be born after all this!

☽ ♉
Moon in Taurus

DEC

24

SUN

☉ ♑ ⚹ ♄ ♓
Sun in Capricorn sextile Saturn in Pisces

Take Christmas Eve to feel admiration for everything you have built this year and all the dreams you have conquered with your good will. A good moment to share your blessings with those less fortunate. Take the day to do at least one act of charity – you will feel even more blessed by the end.

☽ ♊
Moon in Gemini

DEC
25
MON

♀ ♏ △ Ψ ♓
Venus in Scorpio trine Neptune in Pisces

Venus has learned some hard lessons in self-esteem
but now you can dream of a much more emotionally
stable and confident future. Neptune helps you bring your
innermost romantic dreams down to Earth. Be only with
those who value you. This year the Christmas party may
be down to only a few, but they are better company.

☽ ♊
Moon in Gemini

DEC
26
TUE

○ ♋
Full Moon 4º Cancer

Full Moon in Cancer, calling us to feel the gratitude of a year
of many challenges but much internal healing and especially
much more FAITH! Believe that 2024 will be even more
life-changing. Thank your supporter group, the people who
welcome you and nourish you with the best food: affection.

☿ ℞ ♐ □ ♆ ♓
Mercury Rx in Sagittarius squares Neptune in Pisces

DEC

27

WED

A day of restlessness and dispersion. We want to embark on an adventure as soon as possible but perhaps some final details need to be reviewed before you leave on holiday.

☉ ♑ △ ♃ ℞ ♉
Sun in Capricorn trine Jupiter Rx in Taurus

Finish your tasks before celebrating, and pay attention to financial planning to avoid last-minute expenses. We are so eager to rest that we can use self-inducement to avoid feeling bad about it! Pay attention!

☿ ℞ ♂ ♂ ♐
Mercury Rx meets Mars in Sagittarius

The last big sales and promotional action before recess at the end of the year. Carry out a big promotion to raise even more funds and finish the year with cash in your account. Send a reminder to clients and friends; advertise your services and wish them a good end of cycle.

☽ ♋
Moon in Cancer

DEC

28

THU

♂ ♐ □ ♆ ♓
Mars in Sagittarius squares Neptune in Pisces

That end-of-year hustle and bustle can make you even more nervous. Take it easy in the traffic – there may be delays when travelling which create even more anxiety. Take a deep breath and try not to channel your energy into a more aggressive posture.

☽ ♌
Moon in Leo

DEC
29
FRI

♀ ♏ ⚹ ♇ ♑
Venus in Scorpio sextile Pluto in Capricorn

In the last moments in Scorpio, Venus understands
how to use her power in her favour. In the
conversation with Pluto she shapes a long-term
investment, something she will start to enjoy after a
while, but which she is determined to make worth
the wait. Tomorrow she moves into Sagittarius and
the world gets small for so much enquiry!

♀ ♐
Venus enters Sagittarius until 23rd January 2024

Just before the new year, Venus climbs off the back
of the archer of the Zodiac and wants to throw herself
into an international adventure. Time to explore other
cultures, other accents, to pack her bags and simply
leave. What is your dream destination this year?

☽ ♌
Moon in Leo

DEC
30
SAT

♃ St D ♉
Jupiter St Direct in 5º Taurus

Jupiter awakens from its retrograde motion and
we feel again the strength of our structures
expanding and gaining new fields. The harvest
for 2024 will surely be even greater. Receive
blessings in these last days of 2023.

☽ ♌
Moon in Leo

♃ D ♉
Jupiter Direct in Taurus

In time for the turning of a new chapter, Jupiter
hopes for even more financial and emotional stability.
For sure 2024 will be an even more prosperous year
and connected with our nature. Happy new cycle!

☽ ♍
Moon in Virgo

DREAMLIST

IN 2024 I WILL...

_____

_____

_____

_____

_____

_____

_____

_____

_____

_____

2022

JANUARY

M	T	W	T	F	S	S
					1	**2**
3	4	5	6	7	**8**	**9**
10	11	12	13	14	**15**	**16**
17	18	19	20	21	**22**	**23**
24	25	26	27	28	**29**	**30**
31						

FEBRUARY

M	T	W	T	F	S	S
	1	2	3	4	**5**	**6**
7	8	9	10	11	**12**	**13**
14	15	16	17	18	**19**	**20**
21	22	23	24	25	**26**	**27**
28						

MARCH

M	T	W	T	F	S	S
	1	2	3	4	**5**	**6**
7	8	9	10	11	**12**	**13**
14	15	16	17	18	**19**	**20**
21	22	23	24	25	**26**	**27**
28	29	30	31			

APRIL

M	T	W	T	F	S	S
				1	**2**	**3**
4	5	6	7	8	**9**	**10**
11	12	13	14	15	**16**	**17**
18	19	20	21	22	**23**	**24**
25	26	27	28	29	**30**	

MAY

M	T	W	T	F	S	S
						1
2	3	4	5	6	**7**	**8**
9	10	11	12	13	**14**	**15**
16	17	18	19	20	**21**	**22**
23	24	25	26	27	**28**	**29**
30	31					

JUNE

M	T	W	T	F	S	S
		1	2	3	**4**	**5**
6	7	8	9	10	**11**	**12**
13	14	15	16	17	**18**	**19**
20	21	22	23	24	**25**	**26**
27	28	29	30			

JULY

M	T	W	T	F	S	S
				1	**2**	**3**
4	5	6	7	8	**9**	**10**
11	12	13	14	15	**16**	**17**
18	19	20	21	22	**23**	**24**
25	26	27	28	29	**30**	**31**

AUGUST

M	T	W	T	F	S	S
1	2	3	4	5	**6**	**7**
8	9	10	11	12	**13**	**14**
15	16	17	18	19	**20**	**21**
22	23	24	25	26	**27**	**28**
29	30	31				

SEPTEMBER

M	T	W	T	F	S	S
			1	2	**3**	**4**
5	6	7	8	9	**10**	**11**
12	13	14	15	16	**17**	**18**
19	20	21	22	23	**24**	**25**
26	27	28	29	30		

OCTOBER

M	T	W	T	F	S	S
					1	**2**
3	4	5	6	7	**8**	**9**
10	11	12	13	14	**15**	**16**
17	18	19	20	21	**22**	**23**
24	25	26	27	28	**29**	**30**
31						

NOVEMBER

M	T	W	T	F	S	S
	1	2	3	4	**5**	**6**
7	8	9	10	11	**12**	**13**
14	15	16	17	18	**19**	**20**
21	22	23	24	25	**26**	**27**
28	29	30				

DECEMBER

M	T	W	T	F	S	S
			1	2	**3**	**4**
5	6	7	8	9	**10**	**11**
12	13	14	15	16	**17**	**18**
19	20	21	22	23	**24**	**25**
26	27	28	29	30	**31**	

2024

JANUARY

M	T	W	T	F	S	S
1	2	3	4	5	**6**	**7**
8	9	10	11	12	**13**	**14**
15	16	17	18	19	**20**	**21**
22	23	24	25	26	**27**	**28**
29	30	31				

FEBRUARY

M	T	W	T	F	S	S
			1	2	**3**	**4**
5	6	7	8	9	**10**	**11**
12	13	14	15	16	**17**	**18**
19	20	21	22	23	**24**	**25**
26	27	28	29			

MARCH

M	T	W	T	F	S	S
				1	**2**	**3**
4	5	6	7	8	**9**	**10**
11	12	13	14	15	**16**	**17**
18	19	20	21	22	**23**	**24**
25	26	27	28	29	**30**	**31**

APRIL

M	T	W	T	F	S	S
1	2	3	4	5	**6**	**7**
8	9	10	11	12	**13**	**14**
15	16	17	18	19	**20**	**21**
22	23	24	25	26	**27**	**28**
29	30					

MAY

M	T	W	T	F	S	S
		1	2	3	**4**	**5**
6	7	8	9	10	**11**	**12**
13	14	15	16	17	**18**	**19**
20	21	22	23	24	**25**	**26**
27	28	29	30	31		

JUNE

M	T	W	T	F	S	S
					1	**2**
3	4	5	6	7	**8**	**9**
10	11	12	13	14	**15**	**16**
17	18	19	20	21	**22**	**23**
24	25	26	27	28	**29**	**30**

JULY

M	T	W	T	F	S	S
1	2	3	4	5	**6**	**7**
8	9	10	11	12	**13**	**14**
15	16	17	18	19	**20**	**21**
22	23	24	25	26	**27**	**28**
29	30	31				

AUGUST

M	T	W	T	F	S	S
			1	2	**3**	**4**
5	6	7	8	9	**10**	**11**
12	13	14	15	16	**17**	**18**
19	20	21	22	23	**24**	**25**
26	27	28	29	30	**31**	

SEPTEMBER

M	T	W	T	F	S	S
						1
2	3	4	5	6	**7**	**8**
9	10	11	12	13	**14**	**15**
16	17	18	19	20	**21**	**22**
23	24	25	26	27	**28**	**29**
30						

OCTOBER

M	T	W	T	F	S	S
	1	2	3	4	**5**	**6**
7	8	9	10	11	**12**	**13**
14	15	16	17	18	**19**	**20**
21	22	23	24	25	**26**	**27**
28	29	30	31			

NOVEMBER

M	T	W	T	F	S	S
				1	**2**	**3**
4	5	6	7	8	**9**	**10**
11	12	13	14	15	**16**	**17**
18	19	20	21	22	**23**	**24**
25	26	27	28	29	**30**	

DECEMBER

M	T	W	T	F	S	S
						1
2	3	4	5	6	**7**	**8**
9	10	11	12	13	**14**	**15**
16	17	18	19	20	**21**	**22**
23	24	25	26	27	**28**	**29**
30	31					

FORGET ME NOT

WWW / APP	LOGIN

PASSWORD	E-MAIL

WWW / APP	LOGIN

PASSWORD	E-MAIL

WWW / APP	LOGIN

PASSWORD	E-MAIL

WWW / APP	LOGIN

PASSWORD	E-MAIL

WWW / APP	LOGIN

PASSWORD	E-MAIL

WWW / APP	LOGIN

PASSWORD	E-MAIL

WWW / APP	LOGIN

PASSWORD	E-MAIL

WWW / APP	LOGIN

PASSWORD	E-MAIL

ANA · LEO

ASTROLOGY DIARY

2023

Dream, Plan and Manifest!

Every day, Ana Leo looks at the horizon in search of new directions, discoveries and answers.

A yogini and student of Kabbalah, she is intuitive and curious about hermeticism and occult sciences; she sees in the art of Astrology a powerful way to promote self-knowledge and human development.

Graduated in Design and post-graduated in History, she studied Astrology at the Faculty of Astrological Studies, in Oxford. She took classes with renowned teachers and was a disciple of the most important Astrologer in Brazil: Mr. Zeferino Costa.

In 2019, she launched her Astrology Diary for the first time, a true guide to manifest your dreams in real life. In the same year, she studied Astronomy at the Royal Observatory in Greenwich, London, and since then, she has not stopped traveling the world.

Spending her time between Brazil, England, Portugal, Panama and Argentina, she seeks inspiration and information, to add to her personalized services. With Astral Charts and Tarot Readings, she's always attentive to the planetary aspects of the moment, the qualities of each person and the characteristics of each group she serves.

YouTube.com/analeo
Instagram @analeo